How to use this book and information
to benefit you the most.
This book is set up in days.
Days 1 -30.
If you feel that everyday is going to be a tough time commitment.
Spread it out to maybe every other day.
Pick up where you left off.
Consistency is what will make the amazing shifts in your life.

It is all about your feelings, so if it doesn't feel good it will be
counter productive. Now, that doesn't mean that some things may
not be uncomfortable...
Change is uncomfortable. But when you have a healthy
Self Perception and you see that because of your
healthy Self Perception you are Manifesting your life on Purpose
you will be Motivated and Inspired to keep going.

You've Got This!
And your Soulfully Fulfilled life is waiting for you to live it.

The 30 DAY self perception Makeover®

www.cathlencminer.com

The 30 DAY self perception Makeover ®

I dedicate this book to my parents for being my first and always cheerleaders. You taught me that I am perfect just as I am and showed me that there are no limits to what we can achieve in this life. Thank you.

I feel strongly that what holds people back from reaching their version of success and experiencing joy in their lives has everything to do with their Self Perception. Your Self Perception is the base of everything.

Your Self Perception dictates the path that your entire life takes and what you feel your worth is… Which by the way, you are worth everything that you could ever dream of.

I started Hopefull Handbags, Inc. Global to spread HOPE to women that have experienced Domestic Violence and other detrimental situations. We are raising awareness that Domestic Violence is NOT OK and that there is help and support all over the world.
We are spreading the word that a Healthy Self Perception will allow you to recognize if you are in a situation that you know is not right and not healthy. Recognizing a toxic situation is step one. There are many organizations that you can reach out to that will support and guide you to safety.
More on page 156 and www.Hopefullhandbags.org

Dedication

First, thank you to my amazing husband, Brendan, for being my biggest cheerleader and reading the early drafts of this book. Thank you for the advice and first run of edits. To my daughter, Tayler, who gave the first feminine point of view on the book through her perception and editing. And to my younger daughter, Carolyne, for the first run of spelling edits (she's a rock star speller). And to my Mom for her feedback from a mother's point of view on both the process and her success with it.

I'd also like to extend gratitude to the Online community that continues to inspire and allows me the opportunity to coach and edify their lives with transformation. In particular, thank you to the group of women that completed my first LIVE 30 Day Self perception Makeover. All the amazing feedback on their transformations helped make this book.

To Cori Javid, for the edits and asking me the questions along the way to ensure that everyone would understand the heart and soul of this book.

Thank you Kaitlin Rady, for the amazing layout and editing.

All rights reserved. No part of this book may be reproduced or transmitted in any form or by any means, electronic or mechanical, including photocopying, recording, or by any information or storage retrieval system without permission from the publisher. Every effort has been made to make this book as complete and accurate as possible, but no warranty or fitness is implied. The information is provided on an "as is" basis. The author and the publisher shall have neither liability nor responsibility to any person or entity with respect to any loss or damages arising from the information contained in this book. Please purchase only authorized electronic editions and hard copies of this book. This book includes general health-related information intended for healthy adults ages 18 and over. This book is intended solely for information and educational purposes and does not constitute medical advice.

Copyright © 2019

All Rights Reserved

ISBN - 978-1081197520
Author: Cathlene Miner
Layout & Cover Design: Kaitlin Rady

Published by :
Sawyere and the Sea, Inc.

www.cathleneminer.com

Table of Contents

Dedication	5
Introduction	8
First Things First	17
Day 1 - Taking Inspired Action	30
Day 2 - Finding a New Perspective	34
Day 3 - Giving, Receiving, and Personality	38
Day 4 - Becoming a Manifesting Master	42
Day 5 - Doing Everyday Right	48
Day 6 - The Joy in the Journey	52
Day 7 - Action vs. Inspired Action	56
Day 8 - The Definition of Beauty	60
Day 9 - You are Limitless	62
Day 10 - Giving Compliments	66
Day 11 - Receiving Compliments	70
Day 12 - Addressing Self Sabotage	74
Day 13 - The Gift in a Smile	78
Day 14 - The Letter	82
Day 15 - The Habits that Move you Forward	84
Day 16 - Feeling your Best	88
Day 17 - Ego Self vs. Intuitive Self	92
Day 18 - Your Body Image	98
Day 19 - Your Posture	104
Day 20 - What you Love about You	108
Day 21 - What if?	110
Day 22 - You are Amazing	114
Day 23 - Your Worth	118
Day 24 - How you Perceive Others	122
Day 25 - Compliment Yourself	126
Day 26 - Dreaming and Manifesting	130
Day 27 - What Others Think	132
Day 28 - Your Empty Space	134
Day 29 - Life and Lessons	148
Day 30 - Forgiving Yourself	140
Bonus Day - Your Self Confidence	144
Where to go from here?	148
Affirmations	150
Resources	154

Introduction

I have a question. It's one that I bet you aren't asked often. What do you really think about you? It's okay, just answer honestly.

Do you hold yourself back from opportunities because you lack clarity? Or do you have a not so great body image? Does struggle with weight loss hold you back? Are you a woman that never has enough time in the day leaving you feeling like you have taken 2 steps back?
Do you procrastinate because it's not the "right" time? Do you feel like you are settling in certain areas of your life?

Maybe the demands of motherhood are making you feel guilty when you spend time and money on yourself. Or there's no time to think about who you really are, your dreams, and how you could possibly pursue them. Maybe you are waiting until everyone else is all set and happy before you finally make the leap that makes your passions reality.

Do you ever feel:
- You're not pretty enough?
- Not smart enough?
- Not like other people?
- Lost inside?
- A bit hopeless at times?
- Not clear on where you are going?

Guess what? We all feel this way at some point in our lives. Sometimes for a Really… Long… Time! So what does this have to do with that first question "What do you really think about you?"
 Because that is your Self Perception! Your Self perception is the foundation of your life. And it sets the stage for what you energetically attract to your

self.

Self Perception dictates the chances you take, the choices you make the relationships that you stay in and the ones you move on from in your personal and professional life.

What is the "trick" to living the life you desire? The answer is to live in the "now". Now is the time to hone in on your passions and take inspired action to follow them. Now is the time to wake up each morning excited for the day ahead. Now is the time to be excited for the life ahead.

I'll let you in on a little something I don't talk about very much. I used to not think or feel very highly of myself at all. I thought I wasn't smart enough, thin enough, pretty enough, etc... I thought that everybody else had it all together and I wondered... "What's wrong with me? What am I missing?"

I avoided certain situations because I thought I just wasn't enough. I would see all of the popular girls at school and they "seemed" to be always smiling, so they must have it all together. Right?!

I had a terrible self-perception, but I hid it very well. As a teenager, I fell into a life of eating disorders. I would teeter back and forth between Anorexia and Bulimia. I thought I hid it well. Young women (and even adult women) are good at faking it when we need to, aren't we?

My mother caught on (as mothers do). She brought me to counseling and I underwent treatment from a clinical perspective. Even with all of this help, it was really what I thought and felt about myself that kept me trapped in that place in my mind. I later figured out it was a disconnect from my intuitive self and my subconscious mind that caused me to believe all of the things that society was throwing my way. I was allowing the outside world to dictate my Self Perception.

As far as I knew, no one at school knew I had an eating disorder except my boyfriend at the time. He really did try and help but I was living a life in my head based on untruths.
I thought:
> The girls at school that were thinnest were happy.
> The girls at school that had the boys "chasing" them were happy.

I felt that some of the girls at school looked down on me because I was me. The funny thing is I always knew deep down (my Intuitive Self) that these things were not true, but I would talk myself out of believing it. That intuition that I was so connected with and trusted as a young child was like a voice that I wish would go away sometimes.

It felt like a constant battle in my head.

Even in my high school days, I was very independent. I started working when I was 15 because I wanted to pay for my own things. As a teenager, I would help others with my earnings and volunteer my time. I've always gotten great satisfaction from helping others.

So, even though I didn't have a healthy Self-perception and was suffering from an eating disorder, I was still very involved and present. Not many knew what I was struggling with on the inside. I was battling with myself every single day in my head, but on the outside, I seemed fine.

I would base my day on how I felt about me and how I felt about me was not good at all. I would look in the mirror every day and criticize something. Instead of telling myself how amazing I was, I would tell myself the exact opposite.

I thought I wanted to be like everyone else, or should I say my ego self wanted to be like everyone else. My Intuitive self knew that I was a born leader. Deep down I knew that I was great just the way that I was. I always had a feeling that I was born to do a lot in this world. I was born to help others.

As a teenager, I was not in alignment with who I was here to be, nor what I was here to do and it was very uncomfortable. We are here to bring out the best in ourselves first. When we accomplish this, we begin to bring out the best in the people around us. We are in this life to be our authentic selves and compliment each other, figuratively and literally.

Here began my own journey of diving into my own Self-Perception.

As an adult, I became much healthier physically, I worked in a Medical Facility and had two part time jobs. I became a fitness coach and personal trainer;

and cleaned houses on the weekends to provide for my children, but I did not let this bog me down. However, life continued to serve up many challenges. I had two children at a very young age and I went through a divorce at a young age as well. I was always working and I knew that something had to change. I was meant for more. I began realizing that when it came to the things that I most loved and enjoyed those circumstances were falling into place beautifully. This is when I truly started building the life that I desired. I began manifesting on purpose. I started to pay attention to every feeling that I had. Every thought that came to my mind.

I started feeling myself climbing out of my funk. Journaling and meditating for a few minutes every morning was once again showing its rewards. I was getting back into my alignment.

Soon, I was attracting the things that I desired that were in alignment with where my path of fulfillment was.
To not write a book about just me right now I will skip ahead a little. I met an amazing man shortly after my paying attention to the way I desired to feel and where my thoughts were going. My Self Perception was on point. (With attention everyday to it).
That beautiful home I had been envisioning and journaling about was my reality. A happy healthy family was my reality.

My husband had a great job. Everything was really going great. I felt at a high vibe frequency most of the time and when I wasn't, I knew how to get myself out of the funk quickly.

Manifesting on Purpose, I would go to my journal and Check, did that, got that, I see that...(More on that later too).

I became a stay at home mom (which was a whole new world for me) and my husband and I were excited to have two more children. While I was certainly living the life I created, I began to get bogged down once again. I had manifested all of the help I needed, but again life needed to change. I was evolving.

That's when the light bulb went off and I realized NOW was the TIME! Why do I keep allowing myself to get into the funks when I know that I am creating and manifesting all of this. What I focus on grows, I know that. I decided that from now on and for the rest of my life when I have a down time, I will know it's a time to re-evaluate and grow. Downtimes will always happen in life, it is how we react to these downtimes that will determine where we go from there.

We were not meant to stay in one place like rocks, but to flow like rivers. We grow within ourselves and spread our wings to achieve things that fulfill our souls even more. Limitlessness.
And boy did I grow and open up things that I had only dreamed of and some that were not even on my radar.

The purpose of you doing all of the work in this book is to make it so that you don't have to wait any longer to know and experience this life's limitlessness. Now is your time.

So, here we are in your now. Now is the time to figure out what fills your heart and soul, that's what you are here in this life to do. It's time to figure out what lights you up. It's time to plant in your subconscious mind that down times and plateaus are a time for re-evaluation, not failure, not the end.

Keep in mind, that as you grow and change what lights you up will change and evolve. Your growth and change will keep evolving throughout your life. That's completely natural and even expected. We are going to get you tapped into what you are feeling, get you acquainted and familiar with your intuition, and transform your self-perception into one that is full of love, knows its worth, and has admiration for you.

I paid attention to the things that shifted in my life. I realized that some things in my life worked exactly as I desired. And those "things" were what I was passionate about, what excited me and made me smile, those things that gave me a feeling of joy.

I was high vibe about all of my ideas and got excited. So, guess what? They became my new reality!

I reconnected with my inner guidance and listened, watched for signs - listened to messages the universe put in front of me. I felt like I was finally on the path to my purpose, the reason I am here, now.

My children even began to look at the world differently. They adopted a glass half full mentality because they were also learning the power of a great self-perception.

After some inspired work (that I am giving you the secrets to in this book!), my life did a complete 180-degree turn. I realized that I am creating my life. I do have control over it. I trusted my intuition and suddenly had the "perfect for me" relationships enter my life.

I took inspired action and money flowed in. The place I desired to live became my home. By the way, that is only the tip of the iceberg. Even the people closest to me saw shifts in their lives. My high energy vibe influenced their lives too!

Now, I want to help you make that same 180-degree turn. Allow your life to work in your favor. If you are consistent, you will see results.

I'm now living where I have always desired to live. I have an amazing husband, four beautiful children, and two beautiful grandchildren. My passions came together into a successful business that I love. I give back through the charity I founded, Hopefull Handbags, Inc. (More on page 154)

I figured out how to create the life of my dreams. I took everything I learned during this period and put it into this signature Self-perception Makeover. I am so excited to give this to you so you can practice it in your life. Start creating and living the life of your dreams. Once you work on your self-perception, your life will shift in your favor. I has to.

It is important to be reminded that down times in life happen for everyone. When it does happen to me, I am reminded to show gratitude for all I have achieved in life. Looking at the good and being thankful will attract the good back to you.

Tough seasons are great for learning what we are all truly capable of, helping us learn how to identify the good. It is okay to feel down but do not set up camp there. Know that things will turn around for you and keep focusing on how you desire to feel.

Because your great Self Perception is the base of the energy you radiate out. It affects your energy frequency, which attracts more of the same energy into your life. Like attracts like! Desire to radiate a high vibration every day and I will show you how.

THIS BOOK TEACHES YOU TIPS AND TRICKS TO RETRAIN YOUR SUBCONSCIOUS MIND SO YOU LEARN TO LOVE YOURSELF - NO MATTER WHAT.

SOCIAL MEDIA IS A "THING",
We live in a world full of filters and scroll through pictures of lives that appear to be real, but are airbrushed. It seems like everything around us shouts perfection and somehow that makes us feel…well, incredibly imperfect. There is no Facebook, Instagram, or Snapchat filter available to really show the beauty that's below the make-up, the contouring, or the carefully chosen outfits, the perfect family poses and well dressed children. Of course, we know that we run deeper than all of that.

But how do we keep up?

The fact is, we have been trading our own destinies and how we feel about ourselves for the dreams and opinions of others. We have been trading our desires for stereotypes. It's time for you to be the very person that you were put in this life to be and begin manifesting your life…on purpose. After all, now is the time! Now is always the time.

We seem to have so much resting on our shoulders. Maybe for you it's a family, children, businesses, friends, etc…There is so little time for rest, sleep and reflection when we have a schedule that's filled to the brim with other obligations. It feels like the only time we have for ourselves is spent in front of the mirror in the morning and in the evening, if you even make time for that.

That time is almost counterproductive because we spend it picking ourselves apart.

> What if I lost ten pounds?
> What if I was funnier?
> What if I had more friends?
> What if I got a full night sleep?
> What if I had the nerve to talk to that person?
> What if (this is a big one) I was just like "someone else"?

If only our mirrors made us look like how we portray ourselves on social media. Wouldn't that be phenomenal? And even if you do portray the real you on social media and to the world, I'm asking us to go deeper. Deeper into who we are and really push ourselves onto the path that we know is for us. The path that leads to fulfillment and abundance in every way.

We already shine like there is #nofilter needed. We were born into this life that way. The real beauty IS in the mirror staring back at us and in the soul within our beautiful bodies.

There is a secret I want to share with you through this book. We have the ability to create the life and obtain the things we really desire. We must first understand, realize, and feel that we are worthy and what we desire. There will be words I would like you to keep as far away from you as possible as we go through this process.

> Words like:

> Never
> Can't
> Won't
> Hate
> Ugly
> Want
> Might

From now on, we don't use those words in the context that describes ourselves in any situation. Words are powerful. They are a reflection of our mindset and an indicator of our future.

I WOULD LIKE YOU TO ALSO SET YOUR INTENTIONS FOR THIS BOOK AND HOW YOU DESIRE IT TO IMPACT YOUR LIFE. This process will require you to intentionally set time aside for yourself. This is something that is sometimes hard to do with our jobs, family, and work schedules.
Put a reminder in your phone or your planner. Set aside at least 15 minutes any time during the day that works best for you. You will need to do this in a place that makes you feel peaceful and gives you the liberty to really dive into yourself. Maybe for you, it's early in the morning or maybe late at night. Choose a time that will work for most days for consistency and routine.

Since we can choose our words… we can also choose our futures. That is exactly what we are going to do.

Here are a few key components to keep in mind as you go through your 30 Day Self Perception Makeover.

Get a journal. It's best to use a lined journal so you can easily reference back to the inspired action you took in the preceding days.

Go to www.cathleneminer.com for the journal that accompanies this book.

In working with myself and my clients, I've found in order to retrain the subconscious mind it initially takes *18 seconds* for a thought to stick. So, be sure that you are spending your 18 seconds on thoughts and feelings that allow you to radiate out at a higher frequency. This opens you to the flow that manifests your desires into your life NOW and brings those circumstances and people into your life that are on the same high energy frequency.

"Celebrate each and every small shift for how amazing it really is."
  - Cathlene

First Things First

Let's get clear on a few things first.

Did you know that everything around us is comprised of energy frequencies? What we put out into the world, we get back on the same energy frequency level. In this book, you will gain a healthy Self Perception which will allow you to combine that higher energy frequency to get what you desire and live an explosively divine self led life. A life where you listen to your intuition. A life where you recognize your intuition and listen to it 100% of the time. I want you to live purposefully knowing that you have everything you need for success already hard wired in that beautiful body, brain, and soul of yours.

Definitions to Know in this Book

Universe/God: As referred to in this book. Most people believe that God created the Universe . Therefore they are as one. Whichever word resonates with you and your belief is what you should use.

Meditation/Prayer: Sitting quietly or speaking to your inner guidance ot higher power.

What is manifesting? Manifesting is another word for creating. You manifest (create) your life every single day, every hour, every minute, every second. How you think, feel, and visualize affects what you attract into your life. This has nothing to do with religion. This is about the universe and energy.

What is energy? And vibration? The entire universe is made up of energy. Everything IS energy: you, plants, money, etc... Energy is both what you are made from and what you put out into the world. Vibration is the frequency of energy that radiates out from you. When you radiate at high vibrations you are sending good feelings, love, peace, and joy into the world. When you radiate at lower vibrations you send energies out that are going to attract things on that same energy frequency - like fear and greed - into the world. When you are at a middle vibration you send neutral energy into the world. (This is where most people are -Plateaued)

Have you noticed that when you wake up in a bad mood, nothing seems to go the way you desire? Someone may flash a super smile at you during the day - and this is your chance to switch this "bad" day around - so you make a choice right there.
You a.) Flash a huge smile back, which elevates you to a higher frequency vibration and starts the flow to manifest great things your way or
b.) Ignore the gesture and all that good energy the person just sent your way, which locks you on the lower energy vibe and feels like a low or mediocre day.

'See? You have control over you. You control the energy frequency you radiate out. You manifest every day anyway, so why not make it what you desire? It's a no-brainer.

It is important before we begin to get clear on the difference between self-love and self-perception.

Self-love is taking time for yourself. Get a massage, hanging out with friends, doing things for you. These are crucial - but they do not address the inside of you, your intuitive self - your KNOWING - your Self Perception and how to recognize it.

Self Perception is what you really think and feel about yourself. It is not what other people think and feel about you. It's what you really think and feel about you!

Self Perception is key because when you have a healthy Self Perception you connect to your Intuitive Self and you know when your intuition is telling you something. And you start to trust it 100% of the time. You learn to recognize the difference between your ego self and Intuitive Self. Your Self Perception dictates how you radiate your energy day by day. And what you radiate out, radiates back at you.

Cathlene's three levels of vibrational frequencies explained:

High Vibes: Things are better than smooth sailing. You feel that life and circumstances are aligning. Doors are opening. Opportunity is chasing you down. You may even find yourself saying to yourself, "This is too good to be true." Recognize this even when the thought comes up. This will begin to lower your energy frequency. Change it to: This is good and this is true. Leave it at that. Do not think too much into this. When we interact with God (Universe), we always want to think "this or better".

Middle (Mediocre): This is when things are just okay. Your schoolwork is getting done and you feel okay about your friendships. You are "somewhat" healthy. Overall, you just feel very middle of the road and feel as if you can get better.

This is where most of society stays. This is stuck or on a plateau. Know that you can go up from here and this is why you are doing this book. Even a twinge in the "up" direction will begin to open your flow more than it is right now.

Low (Lessons): Here, you are mainly feeling down, anxious, depressed. You feel as if nothing is going your way. Now, it is time to recognize that you are on a low energy frequency vibration and the thoughts you have must change.

The changed thoughts will lead to changed feelings, which will, in turn, get your energy frequency vibrations going in the "up" direction. This is when being in the middle of a low and mediocre energy frequency is OK. You are headed in the right direction.

Just as stated in the Mediocre energy frequency vibration; Even a twinge in the "up" vibrational direction is a great start!

Your feelings are a good indicator of where your vibration is set. Now, I'm not saying you're not going to have bad days or even bad feelings. That's not really what I'm talking about here (though it still very much matters!) In this case, we are talking about our general feeling about outcomes.

Focusing on positive outcomes, positive interactions, and positive opportunities and being excited about the future will yield that higher vibe you are looking for and attract solutions, great people, and great circumstances. Ever notice that the people that have a "nothing good ever happens...or... nothing works out" attitude generally do live a life where nothing good happens or nothing works out for them? Where your focus lies is generally what we can expect (what you focus on grows).

You will notice that instead of the word want... I will be using the word desire...Why? Quite simply, when you say want you are putting out to the universe that you want something. So, you will get just that...Still wanting it.

When you put out there desire... It has love and a feeling of gratitude for something you know is coming your way.

Secret Manifesting Tip

If you "want" something, you will get just that...
Wanting it...

Instead, use the word desire and feel
what it is like to experience it.
Gain a knowing that you know its happening.

Cathlene's Bubble Theory:

A Must for Every Day,
Place a clear bubble around you every morning visually. This bubble lets positivity in and the negative feeling and vibrations to bounce right off and dissolve into the Universe.

You will visually imagine those negative, not so great feelings and thoughts bounce off of your bubble and dissolve into the Universe.

After your quiet sitting time actually imagine a clear bubble surrounding you. Put Sparkles in it, flowers, whatever feels right to you. Imagine it soft and bouncy. When you encounter a negative person or comment through out the day do not let it in. Visualize it bouncing off of your bubble and dissolving in to the Universe. You do not need it... it is not serving you... You have let it go.

> My Clear Bubble allows me to stay on a higher energy vibration every day.
>
> I make sure it surrounds me everyday before I walk into a meeting or any type event.
>
> -Sue

Notes

Notes

Journaling

Journaling will be a huge fulfilling routine while you go through each day outlined in this book. Writing things down serves multiple purposes and also requires using different parts of your brain, therefore, retraining your subconscious mind at a faster, more efficient pace. Start this book with a brand new journal. Make it colorful and fun and a true expression of the fabulous you. Or you can purchase the Manifesting Magic Journal at catheneminer.com/shop

#1) *Aligning yourself for success...*

When you write down your feelings and emotions or your dreams and aspirations, you are aligning yourself in a multidimensional way to attain what you desire. Visually, mentally, and physically.

Writing down fears, anxieties, or issues you might have gives you the opportunity to see them and then let them go. It will bring awareness to what may be holding you back. It will also allow you to switch certain thought patterns around that are not serving you.

#2) *Telling the Universe that you're ready...*

When you put forth an action with a clear intention, the Universe immediately gets to work to assist you. Meeting you halfway. Whether it's getting something you desire or changing a negative mindset. By getting a journal (or even putting together a vision board) and writing in it, you are setting energy in motion towards what you really desire.

When you write down what you desire throughout this process, make sure that you are truly tapping into the feelings that go along with it. For example, if what you desire is to get your business up and growing, write down

what it's going to feel like being successful. What would success look and feel like to you? How much money are bringing in and again more importantly how does that make you feel?
Exciting, right!??

#3) *Letting go…*
Through journaling, you are able to let go of emotions and/or even begin the process of forgiveness or start a process of healing. Your intentions should always be to let go and receive what is aligned for you. When you are aware of your emotions and feelings and begin to harness them as tools to win instead of things that bring you down, you empower yourself and give yourself permission to not be afraid of what you may perceive as "negative."

Think of emotions as nerve endings in your body. If it did not hurt to touch a stove top, we wouldn't know that it is harmful to our hands. Sometimes, we must feel negative emotions so we can pinpoint an area that needs to be worked on or healed within ourselves. Sometimes, negative emotions are alerting us that a situation is not good for us or even that a relationship no longer has a purpose in our lives.

Letting go of these emotions through journaling allows you to process through their meaning and also to not be afraid of sadness, grief, or even anger. It's okay to feel negative feelings, but we don't set our camp there. We converse with them, ask God or our angels for guidance, and allow ourselves to be guided towards resolution.

#4) Visualizing
Visualizing is key in this process. Your subconscious mind does not know the difference between what is real and what is not. By visualizing your desires and visualizing yourself already in that place and feeling those feelings, you are opening your flow wide open to receive those things or something that is better aligned for your purpose.

> Journaling has truly changed my life.
> I look forward to it every morning.
> -Cindy

Affirm your life, own it and be proud…

Accept where you are right now in your life. Accept the reality where you are and know that you have all of the power to change it.
Acknowledge all that has happened in the past, accept that those things have led you to where you are right now. Reading this book. Doing the Inspired Action. Changing your life and opening your flow for your desires to freely come your way. Own your story. Own your past, your present, and get ready to own the life you are manifesting on purpose.

You are worthy… You are limitless…

You are worthy of the best life you could ever imagine. You are worthy of happiness, success, and people that love and respect you in your life. Through this process, you'll realize that you are worthy of more than what you can even imagine! Yes, you!

Each one of us has the ability and capability to receive the blessings and abundance stored up and planned for us, but in order to open the door to that abundance, we must have our feelings and vibrations aligned to them. Feeling unworthy or undeserving blocks that flow.

Working on your Self Perception is the base of this process. How you feel and think about yourself shapes your reality. This is why the first step to really creating (manifesting) your life on purpose first starts within.

Think of abundance as a gift that is wrapped up at a terrific party. If you never open it, you will never receive it. You won't enjoy that one gift that you've been really thinking of. Think of a positive self-perception as opening up that gift. Tearing the wrapping apart with excitement.

Think to yourself and say out loud:
I am worthy of wonderful things!
I am worthy of abundance!
I am worthy of health!
I am worthy of beautiful friendships!
I am worthy of my goals!
I am worthy of my dreams!
I am worthy of financial freedom!

As you are saying these affirmations, visualize each one of the uniquely for you. Visualize and feel that wonderful thing or circumstance and so on...

See page 152 for more affirmations.

Be Without Fear

Fear is the main component that blocks us from the destiny we absolutely deserve and should have. Fear is comprised of many things. Sometimes fear happens because of the bad things we have experienced in our past, things we have witnessed happen to others, or not so great things that people have told us about.

Fear is lying to us...

Fear tells us we are not good enough, not smart enough, not attractive enough, not wealthy enough, the list can go on. The truth is, we are enough. That is what this book is all about. It's about removing the filters and the fear and walking fully into life equipped with exactly what we need that will fill us soulfully.

What to do when you feel that others are saying you can not do it or have it? Or they say you're dreaming too big?

> First off there is never anything too big. Dream big and then dream some more...

Sometimes it will be the people closest to you that we feel are not supportive or they are telling us that they do not think we can do attain such a goal or dream. Keep in mind that sometimes it's from their fear. Their fear for you. Sometimes the people that love us the most have such a protective feeling that they do not want us to get hurt or fail.

That's okay. They are allowed to have those feelings. But, that is their feeling, their emotion, you do not have to take it on. Send love energetically to that person knowing that they are coming from a place of love. Do not give any more thoughts to their emotion of fear.

You will also have some that are coming from a place of jealousy. Jealousy and comparison are negative energy vibration. Let that bounce off of your clear bubble for sure.

So, now…

To get the most out of this book and to shift your self-perception you need to put yourself first. This isn't selfish. You're more helpful to everyone else around you when you put yourself first. When you are connecting, aligning and working on you, you are radiating out at a higher energy frequency. The people around you begin to feel it too! This is not ego driven at all. In fact, it's the opposite, so never feel like you are being selfish for putting yourself first. It's a win-win for everyone. Everything that you will be doing is for the highest good for all.

After all, it's the people in this world that take care of themselves first and that have a healthy Self Perception that are able to help others and change the world for the better.

How does working on yourself and your Self Perception allow you radiate out a higher energy frequency?

You radiate out at a higher energy frequency level because your needs have been met, you feel great about you and you know that you are limitless. You have spent the time on nurturing you. Imagine that every time you do something for someone else or take inspired action towards a goal, that you are overflowing from a full cup, not pouring out. Everyone around you will notice a change. Sometimes they are not even sure what's different, they just know that something is and it's pretty amazing.

You will also notice that some of the people you are closest to are shifting their lives as well for the better. Your energies are radiating out so strong that it is having a compound effect. This is the win-win I spoke about. You may notice that some people are drifting away (more on this below). This can be hard sometimes because we love our friends and the relationships we have in our lives. And even the toxic relationships are sometimes an uncomfortable comfort. But that does not mean it aligned with your path and purpose.

How relationships may change when you put out this "new positive energy," and how to handle it.

Relationships may change when you put out this "new positive energy". You may notice that some people begin to inch away when you radiate at a higher energy level. They know something changed but they just can't pinpoint what's different. They aren't sure why but they feel a bit uncomfortable.
You are radiating out at a higher energy frequency and they are no longer aligned with the same energy as you. Why? Because you are focused on more of the positive. Why? You are a cup half full. You are more secure.

They are no longer aligned with the same energy that you are. You are more secure, confident, and purposefully driven than you were before.

People that are typically negative don't want to feel alone in their negativity. So, when you all of a sudden are not interested in feeding into their negativity and having a pity party with them, those people will start inching away. If you find that some of your friends are becoming more distant, do a little happy dance. This is something that I personally love, because it allows you to weed out negativity in your life without too much effort, just by following your intuition…!

This is happening so that your desires begin to align. Do not question it.

Don't resist and try to fix or bring those people closer.

However, you may, in fact, be the very person that lights the way for the others around you by inspiring them to look inward and make positive shifts in their lives even if it's after they have inched away.

This is the universe getting you where you are meant to be and making room. Trust the process.

Consistency is key. As long as you make this a priority every day - with consistency - you will shift your life.

Trust the process.

How much time will this take? This only takes 10 or 15 minutes out of your entire day! It's so worth it. When you see amazing results they motivate you to keep on going. You'll see changes in your life that you never imagined.

The changes begin around you. Circumstances and people will astound you. And all these miracles motivate you to keep going.

Secret Manifesting Tip

Before you get out of bed each day get into the feeling place of something you desire....

What does it look like?
What does it smell like?
What does it feel like.
Stay there for 2 minutes...

You are opening your flow.

Day 1
Taking Inspired Action

The first entry in your journal for this 30 Day Makeover will be: What do you think about yourself and your physical appearance? Positive or negative, just let it flow out of you and onto the paper. Don't stop writing. Do not question what you are writing.

It might be hard for you to do this at first. After all, we are our harshest critics. Also, other young women (even our friends) are very hard on the people around them sometimes too. We all have experienced dirty looks, betrayal in friendships, and constant comparison. It can be hard to be real with ourselves when we feel like we can't be real with others without risking getting hurt. Remember this though, we want to look and feel good for ourselves only. This journey is for you!

The most important part of your writing process during this entry (and all entries) is to understand that during this time there is no judgment. Everything you write in this journal belongs to you and it is beautiful. Even the not so great truths that you express. The important thing to remember is that you are flowering. You are unfolding. You are exploding with all of the greatness that has been locked inside!

After you have written everything down, take a little break and take deep breaths. Once you feel centered, return to the entry and begin changing over your statements and looking at them from a glass half full mentality. Taking the time to change over your statements is a crucial part of the success of this program - and essential to nurturing a positive self-perception.

This retrains your subconscious mind. Consistency and repetition, along with visualizing and feeling as if you are already in these places and situations, is very important.

The brain is complex but very simple...Like every muscle. It does exactly what you tell it to do.

Change Over Statements

Here are a few examples of how change over statements may look:

I am not worthy/I am not deserving:
I so deserve this life that I live. I was put in this life for a unique reason. I am here to experience all of the amazing opportunities that come my way.

I'm not liked sometimes (others are jealous - misery likes company):
The right people are put in my life at the right times. I let go of the ones not meant to be in my life any longer to make room for the amazing people that are on the way.

I am fat:
I am in the exact place I am meant to be right now in this life and I am taking inspired action to feel good again.

I am not healthy:
My body is headed in a healthy direction and I take inspired action to be well. It feels amazing.

I am here for you if you need a little more guidance on changing over statements. You have access to this video:

> Go to https://www.cathleneminer.com/30day where I explain how to change over your statements.

We all have areas to work on about how we think about ourselves. This process gets us closer to pinpointing those concerns.

To fix anything, we first need to know what needs fixing!

> "If it doesn't make you FEEL GOOD, CHANGE it."
> - Cathlene

Notes

Notes

Day 2
Finding a New Perspective

As humans, we sometimes adjust ourselves to fit into a mold set before us and most of the time we feel like we somehow come up lacking. Social media, society, parent groups, and sometimes even our families put a lot of pressure on us to be a reflection of what they think we should be instead of encouraging us to be who we really are.

We find ourselves constantly comparing ourselves to others' bodies, to their perfect teeth, perfect families, perfect jobs, perfect significant others, and their perfect outfits even when we know that those pictures and posts are just a snapshot of real life. And they are a very airbrushed version at that.

Today, first rewrite the changed over statements from yesterday in your journal. Again, be sure to visualize and feel the changed over statements as if they are already your reality. Going forward, you'll build every day on what you wrote the day before - unless instructed otherwise.

What do you (not others) like about you?
What do you like about your facial features? You know there is something! There's at least one thing that you're grateful for every time you look at your face in the mirror. Find it and make a list. It's important for us to focus on what we, ourselves, love about us. It doesn't matter what anybody else thinks or says because it's not their body and it's not their life.

We are all unique. Taking the time to celebrate even the smallest part of your uniqueness brings that feature to the forefront. This allows you to be grateful every time you look in the mirror. Every time you walk into a room. When you start every day off grateful for a unique part of your appearance, you raise your vibrational energy. When you raise your energy vibrations, you radiate a higher energy frequency and you open the flow for those "things" and situations you desire to come your way.

Now, write about a physical feature you love on your face. It could be your nose, eyes, lips, freckles, teeth, eyes or skin. It can be anything, however small, that brings joy or a good feeling into your consciousness.

Today's Inspired Action

Get your journal.

Now, write about a physical feature you love on your face. If you are having a hard time with this, look back on those positive self-affirmations. Positive self-talk exercises are incredibly powerful and helpful. Talk and visualize.

Visualize this. Be thankful for it...Talk about it to yourself....Really feel it!

Examples:

I love my eyes. They are the windows to my soul.
I love my freckles. They always give me a golden glow.
I love the way my eyes crinkle when I laugh. I know it's there and reflects my happiness.

> "Your day will follow the way the corners of your mouth turn."
> - Unknown

Notes

Notes

Day 3
Giving, Receiving, & Personality

So, now that you pinpointed some things to work on and you took inspired action with some great things about yourself, it's time to dive in further.

Keep on Going. We were all put on this earth and in this life to give and receive love. A misalignment may come when we habitually always give love outwardly without giving enough inwardly to ourselves.

Today, think about a part of your personality that you love while keeping in mind that you must maintain boundaries. So, let's cover a trait that a lot of women have by nature.

Giving. Giving is most likely a part of your personality. Yes, it's a great trait, but do you give too much? Do people "expect" you to give, give, and give? You must have boundaries with everything, even good things! Any great trait that we have about our personality still must have boundaries.

It's OK to say "NO." If it doesn't feel right, rethink it. Rethink it before you "over" give or "over" share.

Remember, not everyone is in alignment with you. There are still some people living more from their ego Selves so you have to be the one to set the boundaries. If not, you will be left trying to pour from an empty cup - and that always leaves us overwhelmed and drained.

I know as women (and especially as mothers) we can sometimes feel like there is a lot of pressure to never say no because we don't want to let anyone down. This causes unnecessary stress. Saying no and spending that extra time and energy on yourself will help you relieve that stress. It will also allow you to clear your mind so you can make better decisions overall.

It's time to turn this around so that you feel fulfilled with your loved personality trait. This allows the love that you have for yourself to radiate out to those around you with no negativity attached.

Which of your personality traits gets you feeling fulfilled and inspired? Now, really think about the role it plays in your relationships. Do you have boundaries with it? You may have to think about this for a little while, but the answer is there.

Today's Inspired Action

What do you love about your personality?
> Do you love that you're outgoing?
> Do you love that you think of others often?
> Do you love that you are hopeful?
> Do you love that you are helpful?

Do you have the needed boundaries with it? Really think about this for a minute.

Now, write it down. For example, I like that I am outgoing. I like that being outgoing frees me to talk to others and meet new people. This keeps me connected and growing.

Boundary example for an outgoing person: Sometimes I am expected to do all of the talking or socializing. All of the time to be expected of something that is a personality trait can get draining. Have your boundaries sometimes you need a brain break.

In saying that, I also know that I cannot spend a lot of time with everyone that I connect with. People come into my life for a reason and I love to connect. I will then find out if I am learning from them or if they are learning from me. Are we learning from each other? All I know is that my outgoing personality allows this connection for me.

So, I like that I am outgoing.
As you write about what you love about your personality visualize yourself and this characteristic. Feel how you love this characteristic about your

self. Visualize yourself playing out this characteristic with the appropriate boundaries.

Tip: Keep in mind the reasons you started the 30 Day Self Perception Makeover anytime you question yourself on your consistency and dedication.

Remember, this is not hard! It just takes a little dedication and consistency. Anytime a negative thought comes into your head, open up your journal and re-read all of the positive things about you. Use the self-affirmation, positive self-talk, and build your self-confidence.

This works if you allow it and trust the process.

> "No beauty shines brighter than that of a good heart."
> - Unknown

Notes

Day 4
Becoming a Manifesting Master

If you've followed along consistently and put the time in for yourself, you already see small shifts in your life. Even if you're just more aware of your thoughts and feelings and what kind of energy you are radiating out. Remember, this is about taking baby steps. Small consistent changes are far more likely to stick. We are in this for the long haul.

By staying aware of your thoughts and feelings, you have a direct map of how you radiate. This allows you to foresee what kind of "things" you will manifest in your life. This gives you a chance to change your focus and shift your day, which leads to shifting your life!

As you re-read, write, feel, and visualize what you journaled on previous days you will get "jazzed" and excited. This is very important as you retrain your subconscious mind.

When you are in an energetically quiet place you FEEL truly connected. From here you can listen and access anything that the universe is trying to tell you. You open up your flow. Flowing is growing!

Today's inspired action will change your life pretty quickly! It allows you to become a "Manifesting QUEEN or KING" and directly affects the manifestation of the life that you desire.

Why? And how? Because in our everyday busy lives emotions and situations can come at us fast. We all have ups and downs. If you don't know how to handle those situations energetically (by controlling the energies you radiate out) you won't get out of those down times fast enough to shift your energy frequency.

If you carry on too long in the "funk" you begin a cycle of radiating out a lower energy frequency. (Not at manifesting Queen and King levels - for sure). When you are on a lower energy frequency you are NOT manifesting what you desire. You are doing the exact opposite.

As a Manifesting Queen or King, you must get out of the "funk," shift your focus and raise your energy vibration as fast as you can.

This a piece of gold and the trick up your sleeve!

Go to Vision

Are you ready...?

It's your GO TO VISION. Ahhh, The GO TO Vision....

This is one of my favorites because it works every... single... time...It raises your energy frequency vibration at the snap of a finger.

It takes some work at first to become efficient at the Go To Vision – so don't get discouraged. Practice makes perfect and everyone's "Go To" is unique to them. There is no "Go To" vision in this universe like yours. It puts you on the high vibe energy frequency that attracts the same level high energy frequencies into your life. This means that you are able to attract all of that goodness faster and easier.

Using different parts of your brain while you put your GO TO Vision into action retrains your subconscious mind. So think of something, anything, that truly makes you smile and happy and gets you all bubbling with excitement 100% of the time.

It could be that your children make you smile every time. Visualize their faces, visualize them laughing, feel their hugs around your neck, smell the freshness of their clean hair.

This is unique for everyone. It could be that you love to Jet Ski. If this is it, then visualize yourself on the Jet Ski. Feel the wind rushing by your body, feel the sun shining on your shoulders, taste the salt (or fresh) water in your mouth. Feel those exciting butterflies in your stomach as you ride over the wake.

Feel your insides light up!

It could be that you are standing on stage in front of a million people singing your favorite song. Visualize the audience, hear the roaring of the crowd, the applause, the whistles. Feel the heat from the lights shining on you like the star you are. Take in the smell of the equipment as the band plays behind you. Feel the joy of being adored by your fans.

This must be something that you can visualize like a scene playing out in your head. It's a place and time to which you can transport to instantly and for a few seconds at a time.

You will then immediately feel a lift in your energy frequency. Even the slightest rise in energy frequency opens your flow. It has a huge effect on your ability to manifest the life you desire.

The scene may change as time goes on - and that's okay. Just be sure that you always know your GO TO vision.

Have it at the ready. Practice before you need to use it.

Practice Makes Perfect

Sit quietly in a comfortable spot. Visualize and play that movie in your head of that "thing" that makes you bubble over with excitement, your GO TO Vision.

FEEL it
SMELL it
TASTE it
SEE it

Stay there until those excited butterflies make it hard to sit still. Get so excited that you just want to shout, "Yes, yes!! I feel it, that's it!!"

That's the feeling we are looking for. The one that changes your energy frequency vibration instantly. It takes you from a "funk" straight to a high energy vibration. It skips right over mediocre. The miracles that happen right before your eyes are nothing less than amazing. Even the so-called small ones.

Do this anytime you have a spare minute (or 18 seconds).

Here is another place to celebrate and be grateful for each small shift and gift that shows up in your life.

Today's Inspired Action

As you've done on previous days, rewrite what you've written every day so far. Keep building on your writing. Be sure that you visualize and feel everything you write as if it's already your reality.

Now, you are going to write your GO TO vision. When you move it from your brain onto paper you shift and retrain your subconscious mind that much faster.

From now on this is your "Go To" way of quickly changing your energy frequency to a higher level. This is your way of going from down and out to up and in it.

Every day before you begin to write, get into "that place" and add your GO TO vision to your journaling.

> "Of this to be sure; you do not find a happy life…
> You make it."
> – Thomas S Monson

Notes

Notes

Day 5
Doing Everyday Right

Let's start today with a super important question and a tip to begin your day using your GO TO vision!

Did you check in with yourself when you got out of bed this morning? What energy frequency were you radiating out? Do you know how to tell?

Ask yourself these questions:

How do you feel?
Optimistic?
Hopeful?
Dreading the day?
Sick?
Achy?

Now is when you use laser focus...Get your GO TO Vision out of your pocket (maybe your virtual pocket!) and go there.

FEEL it
SMELL it
TASTE it
SEE it

Hold it, stay there for at least 18 seconds but preferably longer. Get those jazzed up juices bubbling inside! Get those great butterfly feelings in your stomach!

Congratulations! You just used your "Go To Vision" and shifted the start of your day. (I told you this secret is golden!) Why not head straight to the mirror and compliment yourself? You are beginning to make a lifestyle an routine out of something that not only improves your quality of life but sends you jet setting onto a path of abundance. You just raised your energy and started your day at the top vibrational frequency. Anything is possible now!

Now that you are buzzing on a high energy vibration, I have a question for you:

Do you ever ask yourself what strangers think the minute they see you? Why does it matter? How does this affect your self-perception?

Because what you think and feel about this affects how you radiate.

I would bet you that if you think they think negatively, you're wrong. We usually don't give ourselves enough credit and automatically assume the worst of what others think of us. This is why what you think about yourself is so important. In general, what we think a stranger thinks is a reflection of what we actually think of ourselves.

When you come in contact with someone you know - or even a stranger - and your first thought is, "are they judging me in some way?" or "Are they looking at my messy hair?" Or (insert any judgmental statement here) your Self Perception isn't in a good place. You're putting yourself down, which lowers your energy vibrations. This brings more of the same. You also send out negative vibrations to that person, which is NOT a good mix.

Let's go in a different direction. Go directly to a positive action. Flash a smile. Think back to day two. Remember that facial feature that you love? Imagine that person in awe of that feature complimenting you on that feature.

Using your day two feature as your Go To for what others see first in you raises your vibrations instantly. And you retrain your subconscious mind in the process. Win/Win!

Today's Inspired Action

Get your journal.

What do you feel others think the minute they see you? Think about this and then write it down.

If it's negative, write down the complete opposite. (You'll rewrite the positive statement in your journal).

Something like:
"Others notice my beautiful white teeth when I smile from my soul".

Visualize your positive statement. Hold it for at least 18 seconds.

> I get into my Go To Vision everyday before I get out of bed. -Jen

Notes

Day 6

The Joy in the Journey

*"My dentist told me I needed a crown today...
I was like, I know, right?!"*
– Unknown

Let's talk about laughing! They always say the best medicine is laughter. Not only is it one of my favorite things to do, it also has major physical, mental health, and spiritual benefits.

> Have you truly listened to your laugh?
> How you feel about your laugh?
> Do you feel it is contagious?
> When is the last time you truly laughed?
> How do you feel when you laugh?
> Are you embarrassed about your laugh?
> Do you try and hold it in because you feel self-conscious?

Remember, just like everything else about you, your laugh is unique. It is yours and yours alone. Every time you hear yourself laugh know that you are doing something amazing for your health and wellness, physically and mentally. Maybe you don't even remember the last time you laughed. (If this is the case - it MUST change!)

Much of life gets to be so serious. We have to go to work. We have to pay our bills. Our kids need to be here and there. What is our future plan? What if (more on this one later) we don't make our goal? What if I fail? Wow!! The list goes on and on. It's easy to see why laughter is so hard to come by in our everyday lives sometimes.

Take a deep breath and acknowledge yourself and how far you've come just dealing with day to day life.

Laughter not only raises your energy frequency vibration, but it also has so many health benefits. There are numerous studies on laughter that show it releases endorphins, our feel-good chemicals in the brain. This, in turn, helps the healing and improves how we function.

Scientific studies[1] show plenty of reasons that sick people feel better when they laugh more. Here are just a few:

- Laughter decreases stress hormones like cortisol and adrenaline in the body.
- Laughter brings more oxygen to your blood with the huge gulps of air it requires you to inhale.
- Laughter triggers the release of endorphins.
- Laughter improves mental functions.
- Laughter can reduce pain and speed up the healing process.
- Laughter improves cardiac health.
- And of course, it FEELS good!

Add laughing into your morning routine! Yes, I am very serious here! Here are some suggestions to get you laughing:

- Read funny quotes on Pinterest. (This one of my favorites!!)
- Call your funny friend.
- Watch your favorite comedian.
- Play a fun game with family or friends.
- And, laugh at yourself. Don't get mad… Laugh instead!!!

. Strean, William B. Laughter Prescription. the College of Family Physicians of Canada. https://www.ncbi.nlm.nih.gov/pmc/articles/PMC2762283/ Sourced 10/28/2018.

Today's Inspired Action

Get your journal.

What do you like about your laugh? How do you feel when you laugh? If this is not already a positive statement it is really important to change it over.

Change it to something like, Every time I hear my laugh I know I am opening my flow, healing my body, and my desires are on their way.

Remember, whatever type of laugh you have it is absolutely amazing. When you have fun and laugh from your soul you create so many health benefits for your body - not to mention you amplify the high energy vibe you radiate out (which in turn, of course, you'll get back).

I love my laugh. It makes me FEEL so amazing!

> "It is time to be on this journey to better myself.
> There is no time better than now."
> - Cathlene Miner

Notes

Day 7
Action VS Inspired Action

Let's touch on always being busy, busy, busy. There's action and inspired action. We must learn to tell the difference between them.

Sometimes, you may think you need to be busy to make life better. You then take action, action, action. But being busy and taking action for to feel like you are doing something is not the same as taking inspired action.

You know the whole running around in a circle thing? Yeah, we've all been there. Knowing when you need to slow down before you get overwhelmed and exhausted is key! Listening and taking note of the clues and messages you are getting from your body and intuition.

When you stop before you reach that worn down point you'll stay in the middle (mediocre) energy frequency vibration rather than dropping into the negative. But you may feel like you're stuck. You've plateaued.

The beauty of this is that you will begin to recognize it. You'll stop and listen to your body. When you need rest, you'll rest. When you need a change, you will change. Honoring those simple physical promptings is the simplest way to read your own daily actions and determine whether or not they are pushing you forward or dragging you down.

Realize that always being busy, busy, busy can actually slow down the progress of the forward movement in your life. You may have the "it has to happen faster fever" (Umm, this is your ego-Self kicking in here!) and it's actually counterproductive in the long run.

When you slow down you can then resume with inspired action when it's time. You'll feel the difference between Inspired Action and action. You will be motivated and even excited.

An Inspired Action is a feeling that comes from within. Your inspired actions have light behind them, passion, and meaning. You approach those inspired actions with an open mind and it's exciting.

Action, just plain action, is the action you take because you "should" or you "have to." I understand, this is life and we sometimes have to take action on things that don't thrill us, everyday life responsibilities. However, even in those situations, knowing the difference can create a place of positivity.

Knowing that you do certain things because you "have to" pay the bills (or fill in the blank) is a stepping stone realization. You move forward from there. Rethink the "shoulds." They may not be as necessary as you first thought. And they may keep you looking at a glass half empty, which blocks and weighs you down every time.

This is another very important reason why self-perception work is key. You'll honor yourself and tune into how you feel. You'll listen to all those messages that your body gives. You can tell whether you are taking inspired action or just plain action. And a huge part is that you will trust yourself 100%! You will begin to realize that you are worthy of the simplest nurturing and that, in turn, translates to manifesting the bigger things.

When the "busy, busy, busy"…" action, action, action" dance takes over, you can't recognize the times you truly feel absolutely amazing doing whatever lights you up.

Ron Carucci conducted some amazing studies on taking action and how people react to different situations and what separates successful people from people that do not reach their version of success.
Listen to my podcast with him here:
https://podcasts.apple.com/us/podcast/live-radio-cathlene-an-ron-carucci/id1445465282?i=1000444373677

> "The kind of beauty I want most is the hard-to-get kind that comes from within – strength, courage, dignity."
> - Ruby Dee

Today's Inspired Action

Get your journal.

Let's take a minute and think about what you're doing when you feel your best. Think about what you visualize doing that lights you up and moves you forward. If you've been in busy, busy, busy mode most of the time, you might have to dig deep. Just know those feel-good times are in there somewhere.

This could be the way you feel when you do a certain task. Perhaps it's a goal that excites you to take inspired action, even though it may be a lot of work. It could be a certain way that you feel while doing that "thing" that lights you up. By the way, keep an account of those things as you go through this process. (Write down the little things that light you up)

It may be a time when you allowed yourself to slow down and enjoy the scenery. Write a descriptive entry about that particular place. How does it feel? What does it look like? Close your eyes and really soak it in.

That moment is when we feel great, amazing, and hopeful. If it's not coming to you right away, it's okay! Take a few minutes for yourself in the quiet. Think about those amazing memories or places and let them come to you.

When you reflect on the times that you feel amazing about yourself, you feel a twinge of excitement bubble up. Let it grow (glow!) from there.

Answer this question: When do you feel the best about yourself?
As you write, visualize and feel being in that moment for at least 18 seconds.

Tip to pay attention to - The next time you take action on something, what does it feel like in these 18 seconds? Inspired? Or stale, just action?

Notes

Day 8
Your Beauty

Every day you've written something new, something that allowed you to reflect on the way that you FEEL, really FEEL, on the inside, about you.

This leads to your improved self-perception. Positive talk becomes such a habit that negative thoughts actually take work. You are creating a lifestyle in which manifesting your desires and happiness are like second nature to you. This means that things come quicker and staying on that "high vibe" cloud is easy.

And oh, the changes you will see!

We hear about beauty all the time. These days social media bombards us with images of what others think is beautiful. We allow this to override our true intuitive feelings about beauty - and we allow the ego Self to step in.

When we consider the definition of beauty, it almost always includes the words "she" and "woman" and refers to physical appearance. It's no wonder society judges women on the "beauty" that is on the outside - as society defines it. In reality, the only thing that matters is the beauty that you see in yourself. We are all born unique and we are all "beautiful" with our own qualities. Beauty is more on the inside than the outside. Inner beauty radiates out like a glow! It's infectious and impossible to not want to be around. It's, quite literally, irresistible.

Inner beauty is felt. When you have inner beauty, the outside is already beautiful. Being beautiful is not a reflection, it is a feeling...Being beautiful radiates from your soul ... So now, what is your definition of beautiful?

You'll notice soon that you do not judge yourself. You become your definition of beautiful.

Today's Inspired Action

Get your journal.

What is your definition of beautiful? Not anyone else's - or society's - definition, your definition.

My definition of beauty is somebody that radiates positive energy I can feel. I truly feel their energies and see the beauty radiating from them.

> "Beauty is not in the face;
> Beauty is a light in the heart."
> – Kahlil Gibran

Notes

Day 9
You Are Limitless

You are limitless...Once you grasp and believe that (really feel it!), everything starts to change.

But, this change starts within you!

Remember your definition of beautiful? Let's think about this for a minute. Close your eyes, focus inward, and think about what you wrote on Day Eight for your definition of beautiful.

This journey is all about self-perception and getting you to a place where you can Manifest your life on purpose. What you think about beauty directly influences your self-perception and therefore what you are bringing into your life. Beauty isn't just about your features or your weight. It is much much deeper than that.

Just know that your size, weight, or facial symmetry is perfect as is. This is something you need to repeat to yourself whenever you are feeling moments of insecurity. It's important to look in the mirror and fall in love with yourself every day.

Are you trying to live up to your own made-up story about beauty?

Society has given the word "beauty" too much power. This one word..." beauty"...could affect you in ways you don't even realize. It may be low self-esteem, low self-confidence, or you may doubt your decisions, you may look for validation for the things and the decisions that you make. Maybe you allow yourself to stay in toxic relationships (that includes friendships) in which you settle for what you mistakenly think you deserve. Maybe you don't listen to your intuition (your gut instincts) because you don't trust it 100% yet.

Remind yourself that you are limitless. Once you begin to believe you are beautiful, you'll have the confidence to change certain things that held you back - all due to your definition of beauty. You'll start creating opportunities for yourself proactively instead of holding yourself back from them. The word "beautiful" has a lot of impact on our subconscious minds, and much of it has been put there without us even knowing it, by outside influences through the years.

You must align two ideas: your definition of beautiful and what you feel about your beauty. When you do this, space opens for amazing opportunities out there waiting for you.

If these two ideas are not aligned, you'll keep playing the less than game with yourself. You'll keep telling yourself that you don't live up to an expectation that is literally made up! Your subconscious mind keeps you believing that story. Please remember that your subconscious mind holds onto and grows stories as long as you keep feeding it.

Tell it a different story. Only you have the power to change it.

Today's Inspired Action

Get your journal.

Reflect on your definition of beautiful from Day Eight.

Do you think and feel that you are your own definition of beautiful?

My definition was: Beauty is somebody that radiates positive energy I can feel. I can truly feel their energies and see the beauty that is radiating from them.

So, I wrote: I radiate positive energy to those around me. I am beautiful.

I visualize, as I write, that I am beautiful. I am visualizing rays of light flowing from me and beaming beautiful energies to those around me. With this exercise, I retrain my subconscious mind.

Society and social media have most people in today's world thinking that beauty comes from the outside when really it comes from your soul and radiates out to the universe from there. If people do not see that beauty in you, then they are not aligned with where you are in your life right now. That's OK. Take that sign from the universe, let go, and move on.

> "Nothing makes a woman more beautiful than the belief that she's beautiful."
> – Sophia Loren

Notes

Day 10
Giving Compliments

You build yourself up and train your subconscious mind through writing. This is the beginning of manifesting the life you desire on purpose.

You must truly know that you are enough. And that you are working toward your version of success. Most importantly, you must know that you are worthy of receiving these things.

Never forget that!

Here is another quick way to raise your energy vibration, a tip for your bag of tricks. This one not only raises your own vibration but someone else's as well.

Compliments.

Giving a compliment raises that person's vibration and yours too! A simple compliment can shift the flow of your day and the other person's too. It's a win-win!

Why wouldn't you do something as often as possible if it spreads positive energy all around? You would, right?! It's also a practice of confidence. Sometimes, we might be afraid of putting ourselves out there even to be nice to someone. The truth is, there's nothing to be afraid of!

So, what do you think about giving compliments? Do you give out compliments often? When you do, do you look people in the eye and really make a connection?

Pay attention today. Observe how giving another person a compliment raises your own vibration - and theirs. If you're not doing this it may be because it's uncomfortable. However, practice makes you comfortable! You can even start by complimenting yourself.

Just go for it! Give a compliment. See how much better you feel! We should all live a lifestyle of building each other up. This is just one of the many ways to do it!

Today's Inspired Action

Get your journal.

Write down a compliment that you like to give. I know this can be very person specific, but there is usually something that we focus in on.

For example, I like to compliment people's eyes. When they radiate out positive energy I see it in their eyes. I also feel it. I compliment many other areas too, but I look people in the eyes first.

If this is something that you're not used to doing, that's okay. What would you feel comfortable complimenting someone on? As you write out that compliment be sure to visualize yourself giving that compliment.

See the smile on their face. Pay attention to how they stand just a little taller and the glow that sparks in their eyes.

> "Remember, life is not a competition. Give out compliments and build each other up!"
> – Cathlene Miner

Notes

Notes

Day 11
Receiving Compliments

Did you give out compliments yesterday? Did you pay attention and feel how much you raised your vibration and that of the other person? I challenge you to keep doing this today and every day. Make a goal in the morning of how many people you plan to compliment that day.

Now, let's talk about receiving a compliment. How do you typically receive them? Are you comfortable? Do you graciously receive compliments without putting yourself down? Typically, when we feel uncomfortable receiving a compliment, the big "oh, that" starts and we downplay the compliment we just received. "Oh, that shirt? It's so old…" This is a way of putting ourselves down and not giving ourselves any extra attention, which lowers our energy frequency, for sure! If a compliment is given with sincerity and taken with gratitude it creates such positive energy that it makes things happen in your life in ways that seem like magic. It puts ease and comfort around the two people involved and fills their surroundings.

When we keep our energy vibration high we see shifts for the better faster.

Keep in mind that compliments come from a place of love. Even if it's a stranger, if you feel inclined to give a compliment there is a connection made. That connection is on the receiving and the giving end of a compliment. It reminds us that we are all made up of energy and are connected on a spiritual level in this universe. So, start by being more aware of how you receive compliments. Practice accepting compliments with a simple "Thank You!" You deserve it! You are worth it. It may seem little, but it is absolutely huge!

It's time to pay attention and think about the compliments that you like to receive and give. It's such a great feeling when you acknowledge them!!

Today's Inspired Action

Get your journal.

Write down the compliment that you love to receive! Remember to visualize yourself receiving this compliment with a simple confident, "Thank you." Allow yourself to feel amazing.

You could even take this visualization a step further and picture yourself receiving a compliment on something that may make you uncomfortable, something you may feel that you are trying to love about yourself.. Breathe through it and accept the compliment while assuring yourself that you deserve this moment and you are worthy of positive feedback.

Every time you graciously and openly receive a compliment, you raise your energy vibration and, in tandem, that of the person doing the complimenting!

> "Talk to yourself like you would to someone you love."
> – Brene Brown

Notes

Notes

Day 12
Addressing Self-Sabotage

Let's take a look at your self-sabotaging habits…

Self-sabotaging habits hold you back from your desires. Self-sabotage is common and sometimes we may not notice it right away. What do you do on a regular basis that you feel keeps you from the success that you desire?

This is a negative pattern, that becomes a habit, and begins a cycle of self-sabotage. By becoming aware of your self-sabotaging habits, you bring some limiting beliefs and blocks to the surface.

It's time to pinpoint them and bring attention to them.
Possible self-sabotaging habits could be:

> Maybe you are a perfectionist.
> Do you always procrastinate?
> Maybe you put off doing things for yourself.
> Putting off getting healthier until "tomorrow."
> Waiting to start "that business" until you have more time.
> You are always reinventing the wheel instead of moving forward.
> You're always too busy to move forward.

Maybe insecurity keeps you quiet when your opinion would be valued and important. It could be that you skip breakfast every day and run out of energy by mid-morning. Maybe you smoke or drink and know you need to quit.

Maybe you exercise too much or too little.

It's time to take inspired action!

Remember, inspired action is different than just action. It's that flame inside that's ready and motivated! It says now is the time! You take inspired action to break those cycles that block you from your version of success.

Today, you will flip these into something positive. A positive action stops the cycle! Remember, when you journal, that you must visualize and get into that feeling place. Don't be discouraged if that not so good habit doesn't dissolve right away. We don't move forward by looking backward. It may take several attempts to rid yourself of those self-sabotaging habits. The important thing is, you're doing it! And just as important is being aware of it.

You are flipping that habit! That one that is holding you back!

Tips to Kick Self-Sabotage

Get your journal.

Write down that habit that you know should be turned upside down. The one that you know in the back of your head holds you back.
There is probably a positive action or a healthier alternative that you can put in the place of your self-sabotaging habit. Think about this for a minute. If you feel that you're not completely ready for a full overhaul replace it with a healthier alternative for now. Then take the next step.
As one of the examples above, maybe you do not say what is on your mind and you feel that you get walked all over.

Consider writing something like: I will say what I feel when it feels soulfully right. And remember by holding the intention you are saying what you feel is right for the good of all.

Picture what a situation (or day) would look like if you did not have that self-sabotaging habit.

Now answer these questions.

> What would that day feel like?
> What would it look like?

> What would you accomplish?
> How would this change your life long term?

When you put this into practice, you are on the way to kicking your self-sabotaging habit and you are that much closer to the changes and shifts you've been waiting on.

While you write these self-sabotaging habits down, be sure that you are coming from a place of love. Do not feel bad about yourself or judge yourself harshly while you think about them. Everyone that has reached their version of success has faced their self sabotaging habits at some point in their lives. The difference now and the amazing thing is that you are acknowledging them, this is a huge step in the right direction. You are bold and brave enough to face them and change them. Not many people follow through because it may feel a bit uncomfortable and they quit.

Let's think about getting over the hurdle of self-sabotage!

> "You cannot have a positive light and negative mind."
> – Joyce Meyer

Notes

Day 13
The Gift in a Smile

Today is full of fun!!

Oh, that Smile! That Beautiful Smile! What do you think of your smile? You may be thinking, that's a silly question, but it's really important. It's not only what you think of your smile when you look in the mirror, but also has everything to do with how you feel when you smile.

What is that feeling that starts bubbling up inside? What is that feeling you feel when you radiate your smile out into the universe?

Now, if you have not smiled in a while… Then right now put a smile on your face. It doesn't matter how silly it may feel. It doesn't matter right now if you are faking it.

Hold that smile for 18 seconds.

While you do this smiling exercise, go to your GO TO Vision. Feel and visualize being in your GO TO Vision. Remember, if you picked your true GO TO Vision, it will make you smile and get those excited feelings bubbling up inside 100% of the time.

Now, how do you feel? Notice the shift in how you feel. It can be very small. It can be on a molecular level throughout the cells in your body. But something is definitely changing. Do it again if you need to.

If you have to force a smile you may feel silly or annoyed. It's OK, I promise you are raising your energy vibrations even if it's just a twinge. It's a start!

Numerous studies show that a smile using the muscles at the corner of your mouth (zygomaticus major) and the muscles that close your eyes (orbicu laris oculi) trigger your brain to release endorphins.

You just realized you need to smile more!

Today's Inspired Action

Today, write in your journal how your smile makes you feel. Write this as a reminder to yourself of how your smile lifts your spirits and retrains your subconscious mind.

Also, write how you think your smile affects others as well. Remember that a smile from you makes others smile and reminds them that they are "seen." You never know what is going on in a person's life, and a smile can literally change their day or their life.

Flash a smile at a stranger and pay attention to how you feel inside at that moment.

If smiling at others is not something you do regularly here is a tip:
Start by saying, "hello." That way your mouth is already in motion. Then flash that smile it will feel pretty natural.
While you are smiling, take a mental note of how you feel right that very second.

Another daily attention to yourself detail you should do is smile at yourself in the mirror. You just changed your day...

Everyday challenge: Smile at someone at least once a day.

> "Everything is created twice,
> First in the mind and then in reality."
> - Robin S. Sharma

Notes

Notes

Day 14

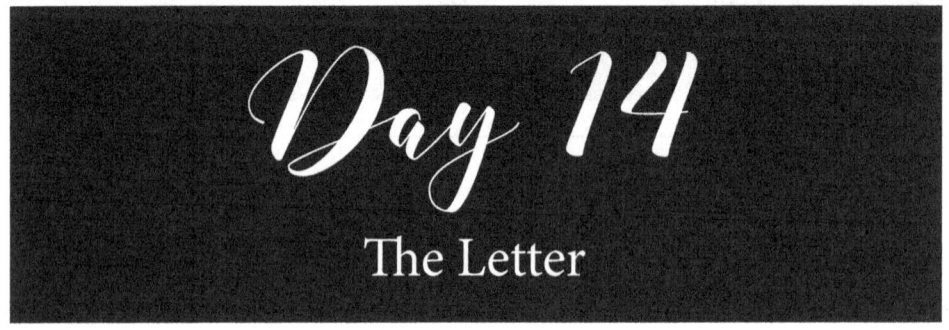

The Letter

So, today is totally different.

Today, you'll write a letter to the universe, God, or whatever resonates most with you. You'll write a letter about what you are most grateful for about you.

Really get specific with this letter! You won't rewrite this letter every single day. So, go all out and let it be as long and detailed as you desire.

Now, there is no negativity or negative self talk allowed. This is all about what you are grateful for as it relates to you. By focusing on just you and your life right now, you bring things to the surface that you may not think of often.

These are such inspiring and refreshing thoughts.

Write your letter to the universe. Be specific. Read it as often as you need to. When you have a down day, go back and re-read your letter. Remind yourself why you are so grateful to be here in this amazing life.

> "You must master a new way to think before you can master a new way to be."
> - Marianne Williamson

Notes

Day 15
The Habits that Move You Forward

How did you do with writing your letter to the universe? I loved writing mine. It was like a weight was lifted.

We are reminded of how amazing we are.

It is hard for me to believe that we are already halfway through this 30 Day Self Perception Makeover! You're seeing big shifts and noticing differences in the way you feel about yourself.

You'll notice that the things coming into your life are more in-line with the high energy vibration that you are on! You feel a more half glass full mentality most of the time. Remember, it's a lifestyle we are creating.

Today, we touch on habits that keep us moving forward every day. These are the opposite of our self-sabotaging habits. We all have habits! Some of them move us forward and others keep us stuck.

Which ones keep you moving forward? What habit, or habits, contribute to your success?

Writing them down - and connecting with them - helps us know that we are heading in the right direction. We follow our intuition and take inspired action. It keeps us grateful for the habits that are getting us there.

You already listed the self-sabotaging habits to be changed over. But what do you do on an everyday basis already that moves you in the direction you desire?

Do you wake up at the same time every day and take inspired action toward your desires?

> Do you exercise routinely?
> Do you go to bed at a decent time to get enough sleep?
> Do you journal?
> Do you meditate?

These are great habits. These great habits are why amazing changes happen in your life! Changes, big and small, in the direction of your desires are exciting.

Be sure to celebrate and be grateful for each one of them. Look and see how far you have come!

Today's Inspired Action

Get your journal.

Which of your current habits contribute to your success? When you write these down, be sure and feel gratitude towards yourself and the actions that are currently working for you.

Write them down. This helps you remember that you are headed in the right direction. It also helps you continue to take inspired action every day toward your desired life.

> "Motivation gets you going,
> and habits get you there."
> - Zig Ziglar

Notes

Notes

Day 16
Feeling Your Best

Yesterday was all about recognizing the habits that contribute to your success.

Today, let's think about something we all do in everyday life. We all have to get dressed, right? Well, we don't have to get dressed. But walking around naked could get us put away!

Some pieces of clothing make us feel amazing while others make us feel less than our best. Paying attention to how we feel when wearing certain outfits makes a huge difference in how we radiate our energy.

Today, I want you to think about an outfit that makes you feel absolutely amazing! We all have an outfit that makes us feel better every time we slip it on.

We look in the mirror and are like, "YES!"

Now, it's worth mentioning here that the outfit you wear every day may not be the outfit. Sometimes, we have go to outfits that make us feel comfortable but not necessarily amazing.

Why is this important and how does this change our Self Perception? Because in day to day life we put the same type of clothes on. We typically do this out of ease and the desire to feel comfortable. To be clear, there is nothing wrong with comfort! Sometimes it feels amazing to be comfortable.

However, let's make sure we aren't sticking with sweats because we feel terrible about ourselves and don't want to be seen. We wear them because that's what we feel most comfortable - and amazing! - in today. This is about breaking out of that "less than" mentality and wearing the clothes that resonate with the highest opinion of ourselves in the moment.

If we never take the time to make ourselves feel amazing we aren't operating on as high a frequency as we could. Sometimes amazing means sweats. Sometimes amazing means that little black dress. Amazing never means hiding ourselves because we are afraid of the opinion of someone else or even ourselves.

When we remember how we feel in those special outfits that show off what we best like about ourselves, we take small steps towards loving every inch of our beautiful bodies. By practicing this, you will begin to feel great in every outfit. Not because of the outfit itself, but because of the brilliant being that fills it…You.

When you feel the "I rock this" outfit feeling you radiate out at a higher energy vibration. By the end of these exercises, I want you to feel that "I rock this" outfit feeling in everything you wear.

So, since we are still in the beginning stage of this makeover, I want you to think of that one outfit or article of clothing that makes you feel amazing.

Why not go put it on and feel how great it is?

Today's Inspired Action

Get your journal.

What outfit makes you feel amazing? Write it down. Write about how you feel in it. Visualize and feel yourself in it. It can be something that you wear to bed, to the gym, or out on the town. Really anything that makes you feel your absolute best! Remember to meditate on that feeling. Perhaps had a glow around you while you visualize.

For me, it is my white jumper with heels. It makes me feel like a movie star! I feel put together! I feel in shape!

> "The secret to great style is to feel good in what you wear."
> - Ines de la Fressange

Notes

Notes

Day 17
Ego-Self VS Intuitive Self

Today, let's chat about your ego Self vs your Intuitive Self.

Do you know the difference? Let's cover a few basics about your Intuitive Self and your ego Self.

Your ego-self is best defined as that feeling you get when you are trying to be better than something or someone else, trying to "impress", or not disappoint. Your ego-self causes you to react to life instead of creating your life. Insecurity drives us to live life from the outside in instead of the inside out. It feels like there is a rush or urgency. Like, if you do not do this right now, you will miss out. #FOMO

Your ego Self is the part of you that holds a grudge or ends a relationship prematurely to save itself from possible rejection. Limiting beliefs and blocks are derived from your ego Self too (remember those made up stories in our head?).

Your ego Self usually is a feeling of urgency. It tends to feel a little bit uncomfortable or anxious. You might have sort of an uneasy feeling about something but ego Self will "trust" itself over that instinct. Usually, you regret it.

We recognize our ego, thank it for the input and go with our Intuition. These motivating factors all come from the external factors around us. Something outside of your inner compass influences you to feel this way.

Something good comes out of it though. You get to learn a lesson. Everything, even what appears to be terrible, is a lesson to learn. It is your mindset, belief in yourself, and confidence in the goodness that determines how.

Now, just to be clear, I am not talking about things that happen to other people. You do not have control over others. I am also not talking about the uneasy type feeling that you get when you are excited about trying something new. It is not that uncomfortable feeling you get when you feel happy butterflies in your stomach. Once you begin pinpointing where these feelings are coming from - and understand the difference between your Intuitive Self and ego Self - you will better differentiate those butterflies to take inspired action.

Now, your Intuitive Self is the part of you that makes calm decisions or excited decisions that feel right. It can be compared to the little voice in your head or gut instinct. Your Intuitive Self usually has a quick answer.

This is where the sayings "trust your gut" or "go with your Intuition" come from. From here, you find answers that not only align with your present self but also your future self! Sometimes these promptings make no sense in the present. However, this inner guidance is your wisest and most loyal companion.

Your Intuitive Self is that which always knows the "right" thing for you. It is always aligned with your path. It knows who you are and what you came to this existence to accomplish. It knows what you truly need beyond the narrow scope of your temporary, external circumstances.

Secret Manifesting Tip

If you are new to tuning into your Intuitive self, try this... First be silent. Go to a spot where you are alone with no distractions. Even if it's just for five minutes. You might want to use things that relax you. Maybe light a candle or surround yourself with comforting things.

Sit quietly. You can call it meditation or you can call it prayers, whatever resonates with you. Clear your mind and just listen. Concentrate on your breath.

When a distraction comes to mind like, "what are you eating for lunch," let it flow by and wait for a message. It may be about something that you have been contemplating or it may be a new idea. Write it down and elaborate on it later.

If you are like me and at first have a hard time sitting quietly, try humming softly (you may have heard of the "om" exercise in yoga practices), or any other vibrating mantra that resonates with you. This occupies your subconscious mind so you can allow messages to come naturally.

It's important to practice this daily, best in the morning, so you can quickly recognize your intuitive self. Practice exercising your intuition daily. Getting better at tapping into your intuition is like anything else in life. It takes training and practice to get better. Once you know what you're listening for, you'll be a pro at recognizing it on the fly throughout the day.

It is important to know the difference between that which is instigated by external factors, that are usually based in fear, and your intuitive self. Pay attention, trust yourself, and most importantly, listen to it. Act upon it with confidence.

So, are your desires yours (intuitive self), or someone else's that you have a need to please (ego self)?

Today's Inspired Action

Get your journal.

For day seventeen, write down what that little voice says to you. Which voice runs around in your mind more often throughout the day? Which little voice comes to your mind more frequently than not?

Is it your ego Self or is it your Intuitive Self? Remember, our ego Self comes from our made up stories. Our Intuitive Self offers messages from our intuition. They come from love, not from a place of insecurity or pain.

At times, we get thoughts in our mind from our ego. These are, at times, just bad habits or limiting beliefs. Knowing this, it's ideal for our intuitive self to be the main voice running around in our heads! This is the voice that it's best to take messages from and listen to. If you are someone that feels like you don't have a little voice running around in your head throughout the day, think about it, be quiet, and see what comes to your mind.

If you like what the little voice reminds you of throughout the day, write it down. Maybe it is how great you are, maybe it is that money is coming to you from expected or unexpected places. What is it telling you every day? If it is telling you that you're fat, then that is not a good voice - and is your ego Self.

If it is ego Self and negative, change over that statement. Go to the video https://www.cathleneminer.com/30day for instruction on how to change over statements. You must retrain your subconscious mind. Changing over statements starts that process.

Now trust the process. Really put your trust in the process. Visualize yourself in the position of that changed over statement.

> "Intuitive literally means learning from within. Most of us were not taught how to use this sense, but all of us know well that "gut" feeling. Learn to trust your inner feeling and it will become stronger. Avoid going against your better judgment or getting talked into things that just do not feel right."
> - Doe Zantamata

Notes

Notes

Day 18
Your Body Image

Yesterday we recognized the little voices in your head and whether they're rooted in your ego Self or Intuitive Self (make friends with that positive ally) and whether they're rooted in your ego self or Intuitive self. When you know where you get your information internally it has a big effect on your Self Perception.

Since these little voices speak to us all of the time, nurturing and training our intuitive gifts is very important. When you differentiate between your ego-self and your Intuitive self, you can control other areas of your life like anxiety, depression, panic attacks, etc. All of these are by-products of feeling as if things are out of control and cannot be changed. We know now that we are in control and we can change anything we want to.

Your ego Self could be a big contributor to common ailments! Your ego-self is the one that makes you feel less than, makes you need to be better than, or fuels anxiety. It can also make you feel as if there needs to be immediate action or you might miss out.

Most people are pleasers by nature. They desire to see others happy. While that has its good points, people pleasing and perfectionism come from your ego self. Even if you think you're a perfectionist for "you" and no one else, that urge is a story your subconscious mind tells you.

"I have to be perfect because (fill in the blank). "

This is why it is very important to be able to tell the difference between your Intuitive self and your ego self. You'll notice that anxiety, panic attacks, and feelings of worry show themselves less often. To get your ego self to take a back seat, you simply need to acknowledge it.

Remember, when you catch your thoughts before 18 seconds, you retrain your subconscious mind to listen to your Intuitive self, your intuition.

We've talked about Self Perception and how we perceive ourselves on a mental and feelings level. Now we'll bring some parts of our body along on the journey. Some of you will feel this is easy, others will have to think about it. You may have to change over feelings.

What do you think about the different parts of your body (legs, arms, stomach, etc..)? Is there one that you just do not love right now?

It sounds simple, but to some people, this is a huge issue.

I've found while coaching women for over 26 years, that most of us believe that there is something wrong with at least one part of our bodies.

It sounds simple, but to some of us, this is a huge issue. That's okay! We all have to start somewhere.

We know that even though somebody else could say it is absolutely perfect, it still doesn't change how we feel about it personally. It is what you think and feel that matters at the end of the day. Somebody else should not and does not have control over what you think about yourself. There is freedom in that!

Let's take some time and think about that one part - or those multiple parts - of ourselves that we don't particularly care for. Let's start the journey of recognizing that we are all perfect in our own ways.

Nobody else probably notices our perceived imperfections, except us. But what we think matters because it affects our energy frequency levels. It's our desires that are impacted.

So, let's nip this one now. We must pay attention to our thoughts and be consistent as we change over what we think about our bodies. We must think very highly of our bodies.

Personally, I have very muscular legs. I grew up thinking that they were too big. I always felt very uncomfortable.

I had to work on this for years until I finally absolutely loved my legs. They get me everywhere I desire to go! I am not that tall and my legs can get me from point A to point B quickly! I am now grateful for my beautiful legs.

Now, think about the body part(s) that might bother you. If there are multiple areas of your body, think about them one by one. What has that individual body part done for you? Gratitude raises your energy vibrations immediately!

Close your eyes and visualize yourself in your mind. Surround yourself with light and think about each one of the body parts you have been critical of. Spend time loving your body and allowing yourself to feel as beautiful as you truly are. This takes practice, but practice makes perfect in your eyes. The goal is to immediately go to positive space when it comes to your self image. So much so, that negativity takes work.

Remember, we must love each part of our body. Let's not ignore these parts. Think about the great things different parts of our bodies do for us.

I would also like to offer resources to you in the event you are struggling with an eating disorder or severe body image issue. Sometimes, we may suffer from body dysmorphic disorder or an eating disorder (usually they go hand in hand). Please visit the back of this book to locate signs you may have these issues and to get resources that will help you overcome them.

If this is an issue for you, you are not alone. I too have suffered and have successfully overcome eating disorders. I am here for you.

Today's Inspired Action

Get your journal.

Write down what you think and feel about the certain parts of your body (legs, arms, stomach, etc…). Journal about each one individually.

This is very important.

If it is a negative feeling and thought, change it over right away. Write down your changed over statement.

Have this thought (your changed over statement) at the ready in your brain. Every time you think negatively about that body part, go to this statement and either say it out loud or think it repetitiously. Remember the visualization practice we discussed. Surround yourself in light.

Think about what that bothersome part of your body has done for you in your life. Remember how we spoke about being grateful? Be grateful for the part of your body that normally makes you say: "Aghhhh!"

P.S. If you love every part of your body then you're ahead of a lot of people. Write down a body part that you are grateful for and what it does for you.

> "The skin you are in is beautiful. You do not have to be lighter. You do not have to be darker. You do not have to lose your scars. You do not have to hide your stretch marks. You do not need makeup unless you like it. There is no addendum or asterisk to this statement. The skin you are in is beautiful. Period. End of."
> - Nikita Gill

Notes

Notes

Day 19
Your Posture

How do you feel so far? How did yesterday go? Did you come up with a positive statement about a part of your body that you felt negative about before? Maybe you've already used that statement today!

Now, we add onto our body discussion. What do you think of your posture? Yes, your posture! It's been shown that standing and sitting up straight (having good posture), raises your energy vibrations immediately. It's also not something that most of us pay attention or draw their awareness to.

There are so many things that will raise your energy vibrational frequency and standing up straight is one of them. How easy is that?!

Why not? It's one of the easiest ways to amplify your high energy vibe!

So, right now, pay attention to your posture.

Are you in alignment?
Do you feel like you are slouching?

If so, stand or sit up straight. Pay attention to your posture throughout the day. Sitting is a time that we usually forget about our alignment. This is especially true during the school year when we probably spend more time sitting than we do standing! So, be sure to sit up straight!

It's such a simple thing to do every day (that we normally don't think about) that helps us improve our Self Perception and raise our vibrations. Isn't that really cool? You open the flow to your desires just by paying attention to your posture.

Today's Inspired Action

Get your journal.

Write down the words below and visualize yourself sitting up straight at your desk or walking tall, with your head held high. Feel how confident you feel and how the energy shifts positively wherever you walk. Feel how straight your back is, feel how rolling your shoulders up and back takes some of the pressure that may cause your neck or head to ache.

Write: I love my posture (if you do).

Or, if you don't, write something like: I now stand up straight, I am proud and confident.

You will now pay attention to your posture!

Word this however feels right to you. Visualize and see how nicely your clothes lay on your body when you have great posture. Feel how open your heart is to receive the amazing things that are coming into your life.

Tip: If you feel that your posture is something that you really need to work on, set an alarm on your phone for every hour or two as a reminder to check on your posture. Pay attention to your posture. Take an extra step and tune into your feelings when the alarm goes off. How are you radiating your energy right then??

It is a small thing with a huge benefit!

> "Be a Pineapple -
> Stand Tall, Wear a Crown, and Be Sweet!"
> – Unknown

---

1   To read the study, go here: https://www.fastcompany.com/3041688/the-surprising-and-powerful-links-between-postureandmood

Notes

Notes

Day 20
What You Love About You

How's your posture since yesterday? You're paying more attention to it now, aren't you? Always keep in mind that this is an easy way to raise your energy vibrations. It's also a practice of confidence and confidence is key! It's easy, so be sure to do it often.

Today is sort of an easy one but it can make a huge impact! What are those things that you love about you? It can be anything! Something about your body, your personality, or maybe even a habit you have, like getting enough exercise.

We all have at least one thing. Even if it is just one thing it makes a big difference when we focus in on it. Some days we may think differently, but that is what these 30 days are all about, isn't it? Shifting Self Perception?

Some people love their smile. Some people love that they are optimistic. Maybe you love that you are generous.

Personally, I love that I am outgoing! So, what is that one - or maybe more than one - thing?

Today's Inspired Action

Get your journal.

What do you love about you? What unique gift that you possess and love?

Visualize this as you write!

So, for me (as I write this) I imagine that I am doing something outgoing.

I visualize that I am speaking to an audience of people! It raises my energy vibrations and gets me smiling! It aligns me with my desires.
I visualize that I am speaking to an audience of people! It raises my energy vibrations and gets me smiling! It aligns me with my desires.

> "Remain committed to success, be loyal to your dreams, it is okay to choose yourself."
> - R.H. Sin

Notes

Day 21

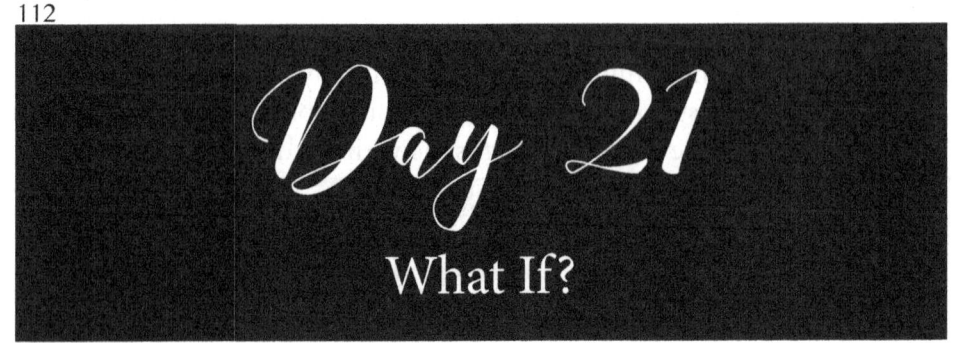

What If?

Today, we play a mind game. It's a little story. Remember the GO TO Vision we had on Day 3?? That something that makes you smile 100% all of the time!?

Go to that GO TO Vision smile, visualize and get into that feeling place. We'll learn to further train our subconscious mind through a playful exercise.

Once you are in that feeling place of your GO TO Vision, think about a "What If" statement?

> What if (write down something that you desire).
> What if I had that house on the water?
> What if I was in that relationship that I have always desired?
> What if I had that job?
> What if I lived in the mountains?

Ask any "what if" that gets you all jazzed and excited! Visualize and feel yourself as if that "what if" already is. Now get in that feeling place.

Okay, now that you are there, hold on to that FEELING. Hold onto it and continue to visualize it.

Now we go back in time!

Go back in time where you felt absolutely amazing! It could be when you were out on the field playing a sport and the excitement of the crowd made you feel amazing. It could even be a childhood memory. Perhaps it's the trip to Disney World and you loved the thrill of the rides.

Maybe you were on stage during a spelling bee and you spelled a challenging word right! Maybe you were hanging out with a great friend! Maybe you were in the kitchen with your mom baking, and you felt so full and excited. Think of anything that gets you back to that feeling place.

Let's get that feeling back!!

You will now go back and forth between the "what if " and the "back then" feeling.

It could be you are immersed in the feeling of being on the playing field with the lights shining down and the crowd roaring. You then switch over to a statement like, What if I had the job of my dreams and enjoyed financial freedom?

Flip back and forth between those two feelings. You'll get all jazzed up and throw open the gates for your desires to come flooding in! It is key during this time not to worry about how these desires will manifest in your life. You are creating opportunities and divine support by just knowing and believing that these things are present in your life.

Since we started with our GO TO Vision, you began this exercise on a higher vibration. By doing this, you mixed up the good feelings! These visualizations are both hi-vibe feelings that raise your vibrations through the roof! We have more than one hi-vibe emotion going right now. Remember, the amazing things you desire happen when your flow is high and open.

But what does all this have to do with your Self Perception? What if …? At some point in our lives, we all have something that we desire and say: "What if?" To be honest, it probably happens frequently!

It is never too late to learn these practices. The positive changes, the promotions, or the relationships you want to experience in your life will usher themselves in. Even though you aren't sure exactly what you want, that's okay. The point is to experience life so you know how you like to feel and how you do not like to feel.

It's much like knowing what sorts of foods you love and which you don't you don't prefer. Had you not experienced the meal, you wouldn't have known what you wanted. Think of these manifesting practices like you are ordering off of a menu and telling the universe how you desire your life to be prepared. You would not be given dreams if you were not capable of achieving them.

> What if I get that amazing job?
> What if I live on the water and I could go to the ocean every day?
> What if I lived near my family?
> What if? What if?

It's so amazing! We are thinking outside of the box now!
This "what if" is exciting!

Today's Inspired Action

Get your journal.

'What if...?' without the 'what if...?'

Let's begin with one possible statement and learn how to think differently about it.

Statement: "What if I got that job where I was able to travel, work from anywhere, and have financial freedom and time."

Consider writing something like: "My job gives me the flexibility to work from anywhere, and I love that I have financial and time freedom!" (Now visualize working from anywhere with financial time and freedom).

We attach a positive outcome to it. You visualize the "what if..?" without the "what if..?".

You retrain your subconscious mind. Then you throw it onto a high vibrational frequency so you can receive the same! Get that flow valve open!

> "What if I fall? Oh but my darling, what if you fly?"
> - Erin Hanson

Notes

Day 22
You Are Amazing

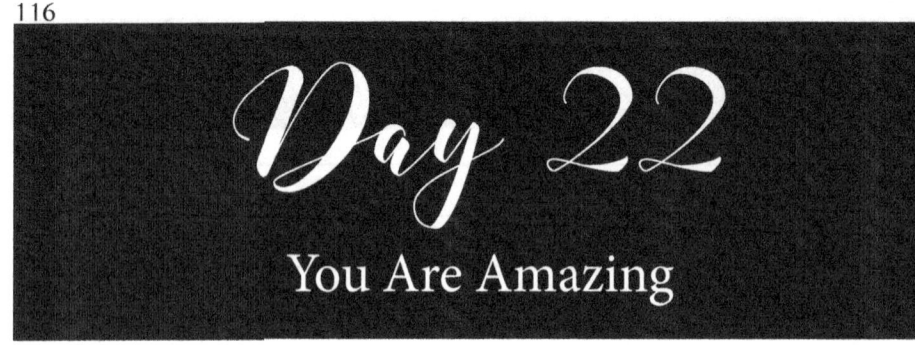

Yesterday you played the "what if..?" game. We mixed up your feelings and got your spark really going!

I hope you had a lot of fun with that. I'd like you to do it as often as you can. You can do this even sitting in a car, driving, or lying in bed. Do it whenever you can! Use all of these times for your benefit.

Get into that feeling place! Get into that 'what if?' place! Raise your vibrations.

I have another question for you. What do you think you do that's amazing? This does not necessarily have to be the job that you do.

It could be that you are amazing at organizing, entertaining kids, cooking, running, scrap booking, anything! If you are a mother, it does not have to be that you think you are good at mothering. I am sure you are, but let's make this about you.

Find something that is uniquely you! Whatever comes to your mind first - write it down!

I wrote down that I am good at organizing. I just am. I perceive myself as being very good at organizing and I enjoy it! I like to organize things, schedules, lives, anything!

Today's Inspired Action

Get your journal.

Write down what you are amazing at.
Meditate with that feeling and marinate in it. You should feel this way all of the time about yourself. You will find that when you do, you are more confident and more likely to jump at opportunities and more opportunities will come your way.

Remember: Play the "what if" game as often as you can! Always remember that you can go back to day 14 and re-read your letter to the universe and get excited again!

You should be excited! There are some amazing things coming your way and you are worthy and deserving of all of them.

> "Nothing can dim the light that shines from within."
> - Maya Angelou

Notes

Notes

Day 23

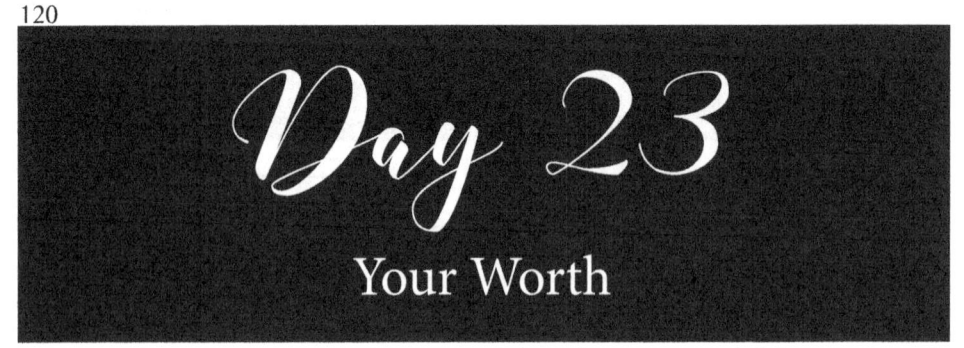

Your Worth

You already see amazing shifts in your life right now. Even if they are small to you, celebrate each and every one! Gratitude raises your vibrations and shows the universe that you are grateful for where you are and what you have right now. The universe then knows you are open to more and will meet you halfway.

Part of receiving is believing we are worthy of that which we desire. Remember this, you will not receive that which you don't believe you are worthy of. So, getting self-worth nailed down is very important in the process of creating our lives on purpose.

Today's question is, therefore, a big one: Do you think you are worthy?

Do you feel that you are worthy of the amazing experiences and opportunities that come your way when you open your flow to receive them? Do you feel worthy of the money you charge in your business? Do you feel worthy to enjoy and receive nice things? Do you feel worthy that the perfectly aligned relationship is in your life or on the way?

You have to know and feel that you are worthy before you see the doors open for the new opportunities waiting for you. I see it so often. People hold themselves back because they have limiting beliefs that they were given from the past - or a block they gave themselves.

You might have had a bad experience in the past that makes you fearful of doing anything similar to it in the present. Perhaps you were giving a speech and you blanked halfway through. Now, you don't speak up as often as you think you should and avoid public speaking. This would be an example of a type of block.

Some of us may feel like we are not good enough, not smart enough, not this, or not that....Not worthy. Whatever it is for you, remember these are just stories that your subconscious mind tells you.

I see people that are trying to do all the right things. They journal, meditate, they're good to others. They have gratitude and they still feel like they're blocked from the flow of manifesting the life that they desire. They still feel like their desires are out of reach and that they are not worthy of what they truly desire in their life.

So, do you believe you are worthy? This is a question that I would like for you to really think about. I am sure you know your answer. Be honest and clear with yourself. This is a step to the realization that you do have limiting beliefs and blocks about what you feel you "deserve."

I find that sometimes people make up excuses. For example, there may be a job you really desire and you say things like, "I am not smart enough for that" or "I do not have enough experience." You put yourself down in many ways.

Or are you afraid of success? I see a lot of this too. For me, this was a limiting belief that I had for myself and it blocked me from success. I put myself down over the years thinking that I was not smart, pretty enough, etc.

Fear is a very real deterrent to manifesting the life you desire. It can attract circumstances and create outcomes that we don't want in our lives. Sometimes it paralyzes our ability entirely. It's important to face fear and reverse it.

I will tell you that once you get rid of that burden that you place on yourself, it is such a huge relief and you will begin to see the flow open.

I always knew that there was so much more out there for me. Once I got rid of my blocks about my worthiness, my world began to open up.

This simple thing affects so many parts of your life.

If you have a business and you fear your prices are too high, recognize where that thought actually comes from. Is it that your prices are actually too high?

Or do you feel that you are not worthy of that amount?

Whatever your answer, what you feel about it will be exactly how others perceive it. They'll see that you or your product are not worth that amount. This is an indication that you feel you are not worthy. And that it impacts your business and your life.

Ultimately, we get what we believe we are worthy of. So, when you know we have a high worth those situations and people that do not align with that worth will naturally leave your life. You will find yourself surrounded by the highest quality just by keeping the standard for yourself high.

Acknowledge it and know that it is there so that you can change it.

Today's Inspired Action

Get your journal.

Are you worthy?

If your answer is yes, and you truly feel like you are worthy, then that is amazing.

If you feel worthy, consider writing something like:
I am worthy and deserve to experience all of the amazing opportunities and people that enter my life.

And if you feel you are not worthy consider writing the same thing:
I am worthy and deserve to experience all of the amazing opportunities and people that enter my life. I am open to the flow. Tweak this statement so it feels right to you.

Make this a daily statement, a daily mantra.

> "Sometimes the hardest part of the journey is believing that you are worthy of the trip."
> -Glenn Beck

Notes

Day 24
How You Perceive Others

Today, let's think about how we perceive others. We may have allowed society and those around us to affect the way we live our lives. It is easy to live more from the ego-self because the subconscious mind was trained to go to the "glass half empty" mentality. We must retrain our minds to stay away from negativity and think more in a "glass half full" mentality. Usually, the things we are quick to over criticize in others are the very things that we criticize ourselves for. So, paying attention to those judgments is a good road map when we are addressing our own Self Perception.

We may have allowed society and those around us to affect the way we live our lives. It is easy to live more from the ego-self because through the years most of our subconscious minds were trained to go to the "glass half empty" mentality. We must re-train our minds to stay away from negativity and think more in a "glass half full" mentality.

What is the first thing you think of when you see somebody?

Do you automatically go towards the negative or positive? If you tend to go toward the negative about others then it is time to become aware of this and figure out why. Be more conscious of how you perceive other people and how open you are to others' opinions.

Do you automatically judge people? Bring awareness to your thought process. If it is judgmental it negatively affects you every day. This type of energy is very low frequency.

Remember, what you put out, you will get back on the same frequency.

I am not saying to be naive and that everyone and every day is sunshine and roses. But what is your typical first thought? Is it: "Her shirt is so unique," or "What is she wearing?"

It is important to remember that not everyone is on the same path as you. Be open to everyone's unique path. Also keep in mind that if you are a harsh critic of others, you may be a harsh critic of yourself too. Think about what kind of energy you are radiating out in that case. This should prompt you to change.

Today's Inspired Action

How do you perceive others? Do you lean towards judgment or do you look for the best in people first?

If you lean towards judgmental, consider writing something like: I will look at people with positive thoughts first from now on. I honor and appreciate their path just as I honor and appreciate mine.

Now, take it one step further. Whenever you first meet someone, always think about something positive that is unique to them at that time. Something like: "I love her blouse, it's a beautiful color" or "His eyes look so caring".

Have a fall back, maybe you always look at someone's smile first. There is always something.

> "Remember, everyone has a story behind them. Everyone is going through different things in their life. Remember this before you choose to judge anyone."
> - Cathlene Miner.

Notes

Notes

Day 25
Complimenting Yourself

The person that should compliment you the most is... you. The only one that matters is you. No, you are not being selfish! We are the base of what is happening in our lives, right?!

I know so many times you will ask other people something like, "What do you think of my....?" We all know we've done it! But it really shouldn't matter. Why do we really desire to know anyone else's opinion?

Whatever your answer is to this it is going to tell you a whole lot about how you radiate out energies.

> Are you looking for acceptance?
> Are you looking for attention?
> Are you trying to soothe an insecurity?
> Are you looking for validation?

We should never let another person's opinion dictate how we feel about ourselves. I see this so often!

If you do ask those questions, do you allow that person's response to dictate how you perceive yourself? Do you allow it to dictate how your day or night will go?

Remember, how we perceive ourselves dictates our energy frequency. Waiting for someone else to tell us how we should feel is just crazy. This is not the way that the universe desires us to work. When you do this you aren't meeting the universe halfway. You stall your progress. Would you tell your child or a loved one to base their day or life on what "everyone" else thinks

I am sure the answer is, NO.

Another thing to realize is that when we have a poor image of ourselves, we sometimes paint the actions or opinions of others in a way that they did not mean. We almost search for negativity in comments because that is what we are telling ourselves. So, when we are complimenting ourselves we will find positive comments and actions coming to us more often.

We must NOT wait for others to make us feel good. We give ourselves compliments because we give ourselves what we desire. We bring in our desired outcomes. By living this way you aren't allowing anyone else to dictate how you are radiating out your energy. A positive compliment becomes a bonus and you'll find you receive them more often.

Compliment yourself more than anybody else does! If I knew the things that I know now back then, what a difference it would have made. I learned many lessons and I would not change a single thing, but wow!

Now I am able to help others too and it's all good!

I know that I am in control of how I feel. How I feel about myself gives me a whole different perspective! I look at this universe and situations in a totally different way than I did in the past - and it shows. I compliment myself multiple times every day.

What a weight off my shoulders. It will be for you too!

Today's Inspired Action

Get your journal.

Think of something about your appearance that you always ask for someone's opinion on. Write down what you desire to hear them say.

Now, you can answer your own question.

Remember it's you that should be complimenting you the most. Fly high on those vibrations! Allow the excitement to bubble up inside!

"Love yourself enough to loosen your grip and let go of what needs to be freed." - Alex Elle

Notes

Notes

Day 26
Dreaming and Manifesting

When we sleep our subconscious mind works overtime. It's usually about either the things that we heard before we went to bed or that we saw throughout the day.

What you think about before you go to bed is really important. What do you focus on before you drift off to sleep? What is the last thing you typically think about before you go to bed?

Relaxing and getting on that high energy frequency vibration before you go to sleep is key. You can manifest and create the life you desire in your sleep (literally) with this practice.
I know to relax and high vibe sounds like it may be contradicting. But, if it is the high vibe feeling that feels right, it is relaxing.

Do you desire to feel different in the morning (rested, refreshed, full of energy)? Use this practice as yet another way you can create and manifest the things that you desire in your life. Feel yourself "being there" that place and or situation that you desire as you drift off. See situations falling into place. Whether it's about your workplace, your friendships, your home, a situation within a relationship...Anything!

For over 26 years I've told my personal training clients to visualize how they desire to be. How do you desire to look and feel? Visualize this before you go to bed at night. Really feel it.

Maybe you desire to live in the mountains or, more specifically, on a mountaintop. Imagine sitting on a bench, hearing the birds, and seeing the clouds up close and personal. Maybe you desire to live at the beach. Listen and hear the waves as you drift off to sleep. Feel yourself at the beach and visualize it.

You are there.

Either make it about you or something that will truly get you excited. See how it changes what you think when you wake up in the morning and how your days flow!

If you are not purposefully manifesting anything specific in your life right now (why not?!) then think of what you are grateful for - truly heartfelt and soulfully grateful. Have whatever you are grateful for be about you since you are doing the 30 Day Self Perception Makeover right now. Visualize that as you drift off to sleep.

You surely have something you are grateful for. Look back at day 20 or 21. What are you truly grateful for about you?

Today's Inspired Action

Get your journal.

What thoughts do you think before you close your eyes at night?

Write down what you will visualize for the next week every night as you drift off to sleep. Remember, it takes at least 18 seconds for this to stick into your subconscious mind.

Then, start every day with an attitude of gratitude.

Be sure to also surround yourself with comforting objects and sounds. Try to stay off of your cell phone and electronic devices as much as possible a few hours before bedtime. This helps you to get to sleep faster with a clearer open mind and also sleep much more soundly.

> "Gratitude is the healthiest of all human emotions. The more you express gratitude for what you have, the more likely you will have even more to express gratitude for."
> —Zig Ziglar

Day 27
What Other's Think

Have you ever wondered about what the ones closest to you love about you? Other people can see the amazing things in you that you cannot. I'm not talking about what casual friends or acquaintances think. We have people in our lives that are there through thick and thin. Those who see us from the inside out. These are the individuals I'm speaking of.

Now, asking those closest to us how they perceive us in our entirety isn't the same as asking for their opinion about something trivial like our personal style! We want to know what attracted them to us, or what quality they love about us.

So, let's ask!

Ask your significant other, friend, child, sibling, anyone that knows you! While you are at it, make sure you tell them what you love about them!

Today's Inspired Action

Get your journal.

Finish this sentence:
People love me because I am (fill in the blank).

Recognize how valuable you are to the lives of so many. Even when you feel as if you aren't doing very much sometimes, understand that just by existing you are adding so much to the lives of those around you. Sometimes we feel as if we have to be making big strides or grand gestures in order to be valuable to others.

> "It is not what we have in life, but who we have in our life that matters."
> – J. Laurence

Notes

Day 28

Your Empty Space

As you've seen during the last 27 days, great Self Perception includes connecting within. This may trigger a sort of spiritual awakening as you raise your energy vibrational frequency. This awakening just means that you are becoming more in tune with a source that has always been there, you are just now realizing more and more of its presence in your life. At the same time, you are learning to use it!

However, these feelings are not always a ray of sunshine. They can involve some painful realizations of limiting beliefs, blocks, and trapped negative emotions. You may be left with empty spaces that "feel" they must be filled. This can be emotionally exhausting, but it's actually making more room for that which will serve you as opposed to that which has kept you in some negative cycles.

Know that you are making space for the amazing things you've been waiting for to come into your life. Those gaps you feel will be filled soon so be grateful for the spaces.

The lessons that we learn in this life are so valuable. The more we become aware, learn the lessons we need to through our experiences, and let go of negative energies, the more room it leaves for an amazing high energy vibration to fill the space. When we resist these changes and do not choose to move forward it can cause depression, anxiety, pain and so on.

By letting go, learning our lessons, and moving on, we connect with the universe by vibrating at a high energy. This allows us to live our best life. It also allows to us to heal ourselves and permanently change that which kept us in cycles that weren't allowing for us to move forward. Once you feel your soul connect, partial love for yourself will no longer be enough. You will know that in this life it all starts with Self Perception and believing in yourself.

Love you for you and where you are right now in this space, is the place to begin. Right now, you are exactly where you need to be. There is more out there. You know that you can love you. You know this life is limitless.

Everyone who has made it to this point has had a situation that has challenged them to think about the path they are on in their lives. We sometimes forget about what is truly on the inside when we focus so much on the outside.

Today's Inspired Action

Get your journal.

What lesson turned you around and reminded you that it was time to connect to your intuition? Perhaps focus on a situation you once perceived as negative, but now you understand how much it taught you.

What are you grateful for about it? Write this down.

Side note: Sometimes it's hard to be grateful for things that have happened in our lives that left us feeling pain, heartache, or even betrayal. Think of pain as a navigator. It is there to show us the areas of our lives where something needs healing or something needs to change.

> "Yesterday I was clever, so I wanted to change the world.
> Today I am wise, so I am changing myself."
> – Rumi

Notes

Notes

Day 29
Life and Lessons

Learning how your brain really works on a subconscious level allows you to truly, and purposefully, manifest (create/magnetize) your desired life and opportunities. More importantly, it allows you to recognize those opportunities to take inspired action on those amazing possibilities when they present themselves.

Maybe there is something that you thought was negative, but you now see it in a positive light?

This is much like our topic yesterday. The reason I am bringing this up is because how we face and feel through challenges will affect how we react and make choices through them. Feeling negative about challenge usually yields negative results. It is important to understand that we grow through challenge.

Facing challenges with an open mind and willingness to learn and grow through them means that we are in control. When we allow emotion to take over and begin to feel like nothing is going to work in our favor, we have handed over the keys. We are no longer driving.

Today's Inspired Action

Get your journal.

This is your focus for today: What is that one BIG take away that stands out in your mind from the past 28 days?

The AH HA moment.

> "Knowing yourself is the beginning of all wisdom."
> - Aristotle

Notes

Day 30
Forgiving Yourself

Whatever is on your mind on a day-to-day basis is directly correlated to the energy vibrations that you send out.

What is that "thing" that you need to forgive yourself for?

Self-forgiveness is a block that we may not recognize at first, but it is one of the most important. Instead of forgiving ourselves for different actions or thoughts, most tend to push them to the back of the mind and ignore it. This keeps us from forgiving ourselves and healing within. Do you ever notice that most of us are more quick to forgive others than we are to forgive ourselves.

Just because we wish something never happened doesn't mean it didn't. We must acknowledge that we may have needed certain events to occur to teach us certain lessons in life. We can learn a lot from the things that didn't go our way, if we just let ourselves.

Forgiveness allows us to nurture that place within us and allows it to heal, grow, and evolve. Think of that something that you need to forgive yourself for (or heal from) and accept that it happened. Give yourself credit for getting through it. Recognize that it taught you a lesson and gave you the ability to delve deeper into yourself.

Now it is time to forgive yourself and heal so you can move on. By doing this, you unblock your flow, open up your world, and see shifts happen right before your eyes.

You cannot change that it happened. So, forgive yourself and take that weight off of your shoulders. It is really okay. It is over.

Today's Inspired Action

Get your journal.

Today, write what you forgave yourself for. Be sure to write specifically about what you have forgiven and that you have released what you no longer need (make these words resonate with you).

You can now release it and begin to heal. The healing space requires zero judgment and criticism. Imagine it is a place of healing light.

Bonus: On the next full moon and new moon, use the moon's energies to help manifest and rid yourself of blocks, limiting beliefs, and forgive yourself for past events. For more information on the full moon and new moon rituals, visit my website.

www.cathleneminer.com/30day

"Self-forgiveness is essential to self-healing."
- Ruth Carter Stapleton

Notes

Notes

Bonus Day
Your Self Confidence

Now, let's think about self confidence and what it is. Webster's Dictionary defines it as: "confidence in oneself and in one's powers and abilities."

So many people credit the amount of confidence they have in themselves to their outward definition of success. How much money am I making? How many friends do I have? DO myself and my family look like polished all of the time? How many likes did I get on that photo?
Self confidence is built on so many different things working together, but the base always begins with your Self Perception, your foundation is built there.

Think about it. It has everything to do with how you think and feel about you. Your Self Perception dictates your personal version of success. It dictates how high you aim and how far you will take it. It dictates what you will "settle" for (I do not encourage settling at all). And, of course, it dictates the choices you make.

Think ahead a year or so, the outfit you wore to that workout class will not matter at all!!!

First, you must know what your version of success looks like and how you use your passions to get you there. The passion you have for something translates to how much fuel you have to get the job done. I know you hear it all of the time but it's so true, it's about the journey.
Why?? The lessons learned the forks in the road that lead to other amamzing opportunities.
However, you'll experience many wins on the way. Your version of success will change throughout the years too!

Taking the time to discover these things is one of the most worthwhile uses of your time in life. I know that you have been inspired during these past 30 days and now know what really lights you up and what feelings you do not desire to feel.

Self confidence is believing in yourself enough to make decisions without needing external guidance and opinions all f the time to confirm your choices (a trusted friends advice is always welcome). Know when you aren't being treated with respect (we receive what we think we deserve). Stand up for yourself by doing what is right no matter what you think others will think about it. Follow your intuition… You know.

When you started this journey 30 days ago, your self confidence may not have been soaring. Where are you now? What is one thing that you can say you are "super" confident about now?

When you have a healthy Self Perception ans confidence, true confidence, you know that the only thing that matters is what you think about yourself. You are 100% confident in your decisions because you can feel that you are aligned with your intuition. So, you trust your intuition, your "gut" 100 %. Your intuition leads you on the path to your passions. Sometimes that means taking risks not many would and living a life that is "outside of the box".

Your life will not always go along the way you planned, but remember that this is okay. When you hear a "no", it is not a "never". It simply means "not this way" or "not right now". There may be something right around the corner that you will love even more! You are still attracting what you need to create the life that you desire.

You also no longer compare yourself to others. You may look up to someone or admire them, but comparing is a thing of the past.

As you go through life, remember that you will make important decisions and set boundaries for yourself. There may be some people that feel threatened by your confidence. You do not have to take ownership of how your decisions make them feel. You are uniquely and beautifully you. There is no apology necessary.

Now...take on the world.

Today's Inspired Action

Get your journal.

What is one thing that you feel super self confident about now? Without a doubt you know you can do this "thing" or this "thing" is going to happen. Have no doubts when you put it to paper.

By acknowledging this and getting it from your brain onto the paper and then visualizing yourself there, you begin a chain reaction of energetic events. Be confident of your position in that chain of events and feel what it's like to be there. As you do this, you raise your energy frequency and align with the perfect path for you right now.

> "Once you become fearless, life becomes limitless."
> - unknown

Notes

Where To Go From Here

Well!! You did it!!

I am so happy to be on this journey with you. It's an amazing feeling to share the best parts of some of the work that has made a huge impact in my life, my friends' lives, my children's lives and my clients' lives throughout the years. I loved the process of writing it all down so that I can share it with you and the world. You will be connected to your intuition and ahead in the game.

You did this work the last 30 days to begin your journey towards manifesting the life that you desire. You can now see how everything in this life is based on how you feel about yourself, your Self Perception and it radiates out from there.

You can achieve anything once you know that you are limitless. Set your mind to it, visualize it, and feel it. Once you do, whatever you desire is on its way.

Whether you made big or small shifts in your life these past 30 days, I am here to celebrate each one of those with you. Now live life constantly celebrating yourself. Celebrate everything, even the little steps you take or things you do. Celebration is a must.

If you followed each day, showed up for yourself, followed through, and took Inspired Action, look back and observe how far you have come. Now that you have a better Self Perception, your entire world shifts in your favor. It is important to keep it up!

These 30 days were an absolutely amazing start but the journey is not over yet. It is important to keep journaling and meditating. Think of that GO

TO Vision that you journaled about. Recall it right now or anytime you feel it is important to keep practicing that feeling so you have it at the ready and can use it. Use your bag of tricks when you feel the "funk" creeping in and you need to get yourself out of a low energy vibration.

Take a minute some days to go back to day 14 and reread your letter to the universe. Visualize and feel it as you read. Play the "what if" game as often as you can (we all love a game!).
It's exciting when you get into the place of truly feeling things positively change.

These are practices that will guide you for the rest of your life to make positive shifts and changes. Spread the word and tell a friend. Allow them to begin their journey.

I created a journaling course and book that explains the steps of journaling for the life you desire (subscribe at cathleneminer.com to get the course launch date sent). Doing the journaling course after you have put this book into practice allows even more amazing shifts in your life (I know! - it's possible!). I recommend doing the course and book. Then create your very own unique journaling practice for yourself.

It is extremely important that you revisit The 30 Day Self Perception Makeover every six months. Revisit it when you feel disconnected from the true authentic you or when the outside world begins to dictate your life.

As I mentioned in this book, you are exposed to the energy of others every day. With the ebb and flow of life, your path changes. Change is a great thing and something I definitely encourage. Just be cognizant of how those changes make you feel. If it feels right it will lead to your personal, spiritual, and financial growth throughout the years.

When you reconnect every 6 months or more you'll have a much clearer view of the path that you were put in this life to take; the path that fills your soul and keeps you reaching for more.

Remember to follow your intuition. The universe has a plan for you that is better than you could ever imagine. You can live it as long as you listen.

Be quiet and listen. Be sure to subscribe to my Manifesting Magic in your everyday life blog for weekly instruction and daily inspiration.

Happy manifesting!

"You are only at the beginning… Just imagine what else is out there waiting for you."

– Cathlene

To keep up "Manifesting Magic in your everyday life®" go to
www.cathleneminer.com

Affirmations

Positive Affirmations.

Use these affirmations as Inspiration to you. Change them up and make them your own. Pick your favorite and repeat them daily. Write them on sticky notes and place them everywhere! Use them different times throughout the day. Maybe have some on your bathroom mirror.
On your computer, etc...

I am

I am important.
I am brave.
I am safe and secure.
I am beautiful.
I am strong.
I am confident.
I am worthy.
I am allowed to feel all of my feelings.
I am kind.
I am creative.
I am imaginative.

I can communicate with others

I speak with kindness
I speak with respect.
I speak with strength.
I speak with courage.
I stand up for myself.
I stand up for others.
I listen with love.
I speak through love.
I have the courage to share my true feeling.
Others do not have to agree with me and that's OK.
I respect others even I do not agree with them.
I am responsible for my words.

Challenges

I can overcome any challenges.
I have a solution based approach to challenges.
I ask for help when needed.
I have support in facing my challenges.
I learn from my challenges.
Challenges make me stronger and allow me to help others.
I can handle any challenges that come my way.

Getting Peaceful and Calm

I am peaceful.
I am relaxed.
I am calm.
I let go of my worries and stressors.
I can calm my mind by going inward and feeling my breath.
I am relaxing my whole body and mind.
I feel my stressors dissolve away.

Working Together

We are all more similar than different.
Each person has something unique to contribute.
Each of us can work together to solve problems.
Together we will create peace.
Together we the world!

I believe I am

I believe in myself.
I am awesome!
I am allowed to feel proud of myself.
I trust myself.
I trust my intuition 100%
I listen to my heart.

Acceptance and Loving Myself

I love myself.
I accept myself.
I am worthy of my heartfelt desires.
I deserve to be happy.
I consider my own feelings
I consider other people's feelings.
I am my own perfect.
I can be accepted just as I am.
I love and accept all parts of myself.

I forgive myself for my mistakes and have learned by them.
I think positive thoughts about myself.
I speak to myself with kindness.
My body is strong and healthy.
I respect my body.

It's OK to be:

It's okay to be sad.
It's okay to be angry.
It's okay to be scared.
It's OK to say no.

I am grateful

I am grateful for what I have.
I am compassionate.
I am generous.
I love my body.
I am grateful for my health.
My body is perfect the way it is.

I don't compare myself to others.
I am grateful to my body.

Relationships

I help others.
I include others.
I am a good friend.
I am trustworthy.
I can be myself in my friendships.
It's OK to be different than my friends.
I am unique.
I am allowed to have all kinds of friends.
I deserve to be accepted for my true self.
I deserve to be treated with kindness.
I can be my own unique self and belong.
I am an important part of my family.
I can disagree with my family and still be loved.
I am loved.
I love my family.

I will get my life's desires

I set my own unique goals(desires).
I enjoy the journey to my goals.
I enjoy being challenged and learning.
I can make mistakes and still reach my goals.
I believe in myself.
I am consistent.
I always take inspired action.
It's OK to accept help from others on the journey to my desires, goals.
I believe in my dreams.
I can reach my dreams.
I go with the flow.
I have amazing ideas.
I am always open to new ideas.
Anything in this Universe is possible.
This Universe is limitless and my wildest dreams can come true.

Hopefull Handbags Inc. ®

Nonprofit, 501c3

I started Hopefull Handbags with a mission is to give Hope to women getting back on their feet again due to Domestic Violence and other detrimental situations. We do this one handbag at a time by receiving once loved donated handbags, filling them with necessities, inspirational notes and things to make women feel amazing and donating them to women getting back on their feet again. Some of these women are staying in shelters and most with children. The smiles and the feeling of hope are priceless.

"Never Underestimate the Power of Hope".
The Handbags Full of Hope is only part of it. For Hopefull Handbags, it is also about raising awareness that Domestic Violence is real. It happens in all socioeconomic backgrounds as with other detrimental situations some women may find themselves in.

Another part of our mission is raising awareness around the world that there is Help, Hope and Support all over at no charge. The more people we can spread the word to we potentially reach the very women that need to be connected to safety. Maybe they just start with a mention to a friend and that friend directing them to us or an organization that can guide them and their children to safety.

Men are also survivors of Domestic Violence and the Detrimental Situations sometimes and they are given the same services when needed.

Hopefull Handbags, Inc. 501c3 believes in collaboration over competition. That is why all events that Hopefull Handbags hosts or partner with provide a safe, inspirational, motivational, and educational uplifting experience.
A fun setting for women to engage with their community.

Hopefull Handbags focuses on providing the knowledge, tools, and community to give Hope, Help, and Support for you to feel inspired, motivated and empowered to create a positive change in your life which affects everything and everyone around you.

Raising Hope and Vibrational Energies,
"One Handbags at a Time"

If You, Your Group or Business would like to get involved or partner with an event message us at info@hopefullhandbags.org

WWW.HOPEFULLHANDBAGS.ORG

Resources

USA

*Domestic Violence
and Dating Abuse
National Abuse Hotline:*
The Hotline.org
1-800-799-7233

Eating Disorders
National Eating Disorders.org
1-800-931-2237

Suicide Life Line
LinesforLife.org
Suicide Life Line
1-800-273-8255 (24/7/365)
Text 273TALK to 839863 (8am-11pm PST)

Alcohol and Drug Helpline
1-800-923-4357 (24/7/365)
Text RecoveryNow to 839863 (8am-11pm PST daily)

YOUTHLINE
Call 877-968-8491
Text teen2teen to 839863
Chat at www.oregonyouthline.org

Australia

Domestic Violence
Dating Abuse
1800 RESPECT or 1800 737 732
https://au.reachout.com/articles/domestic-violence-support

Eating Disorders
https://thebutterflyfoundation.org.au/our-services/helpline/Call 1800 ED HOPE (1800 33 4673)

Suicide Life Line
https://www.lifeline.org.au/
https://www.lifeline.org.au/get-help/topics/lifeline-services

KidsHelpLine
Kidshelpline.com.au
1800 55 1800

United Kingdom

Domestic Violence/Dating Abuse
0808 2000 247

Eating Disorders
https://www.beateatingdisorders.org.uk/support services
0808 801 0711

Suicide Life Line
Helpline: 01708 765200
https://www.supportline.org.uk/problems/suicide/

Alcohol and Drug Helpline
https://www.supportline.org.uk/problems/drugs/

Canada

Domestic Violence/Dating Abuse
1-800-579-2888
Eating Disorders
http://nedic.ca/

http://www.kidshelpphone.ca
1-800-668-6868

Suicide Life Line
http://www.crisisservicescanada.ca/
18334564566

Chat via text: 45645

If you are in need of a different resources message us at
facebook.com/Hopefullhandbags
so we can connect you with the support line near you.

The self perception Makeover Method

Coming!! Soon A 6 Week Course lead by Cathlene!

Love, Cathlene

Get inspiration and ways to
Manifest Magic in your Everyday Life right to your inbox.
www.cathleneminer.com